Letts

KEY STAGE 3
(AGE 11-14)

ICT

Revise KS3

Information and Communication Technology

Authors - Max Begley and David Sadler

Contents

ICT at Key Stage 3

Introduction to KS3 information and communication technology

This ICT study guide has been written specifically to provide complete coverage of the ICT National Curriculum at Key Stage 3. The content has been carefully matched to the National Strategy Framework for teaching ICT capability: Years 7, 8 and 9.

This is an important stage in your education because it lays the foundation for the ICT you will need at Key Stage 4 whether you are studying GCSE ICT, applied GCSE ICT, Key Skills, or any other qualification, or whether you will only be using it to support your other subjects. The National Curriculum requires all 14-year-olds to cover certain aspects of ICT at Key Stage 4 in one way or another.

ICT capability in Key Stage 3

ICT capability involves information gathering, presentation and technical processing skills, underpinned by an understanding of key concepts related to the nature of information technology. It includes but is broader than a set of technical competences in common software applications.

The aim is to ensure that by the end of Key Stage 3 all pupils can use ICT securely, creatively and independently, are confident enough to keep their skills up-to-date and are able to generalise from their experiences.

Key Stage 3 ICT is broken down into four themes:

1 Finding things out

This is about understanding what makes information, about motivating enquiry and making independent study more focused and productive.

2 Developing ideas and making things happen

This is about what users can do with information once it has been collected. It is about how to transform, develop or display the information effectively.

3 Exchanging and sharing information

This is about the process of communication and how it helps to form communities, transmit values, experiences and traditions, and expand horizons.

4 Reviewing, modifying and evaluating work as it progresses

This theme is integrated with the other three themes. The evaluation skills are required whatever you are working on in ICT and therefore there is no discrete section for this theme in the book, it is included throughout.

How this book will help

From 2004, SATs tests are being introduced, first as a pilot to a small number of schools, eventually becoming compulsory for all students at the end of Key Stage 3. Most students will achieve an overall level of 5 or 6. The results will be used by the government to check whether standards of achievement are rising nationally and by people who make comparisons of the achievements of pupils in different schools.

Successful study

This book should be used throughout Key Stage 3 to help you make sure you know and understand the key facts and issues as you go along. You should then be able to use this information to help you answer questions.

Success in school depends on regular planned work over a period of time rather than panic bursts of very hard work just before an examination.

If you develop the habit of regularly reviewing the work you have done in school, and making sure you understand it, it is less likely to cause you severe problems as the SATs approach.

Features in the study guide

Chapters 1, 4 and 7 cover the work you are likely to study in Year 7.

Chapters 2, 5 and 8 cover the work you are likely to study in Year 8.

Chapters 3, 6 and 9 cover the work you are likely to study in Year 9.

Progress checks

At the end of each chapter there are progress check questions. These are not the type that you will meet in the SATs but are there to help you check what you have learned as you go through the topics in the book.

Skills checks

At the end of each chapter there is a skills check. This is designed to remind you of the skills used in that chapter so that you can quickly go through them and check whether you are competent at each skill. The answers are not provided – you need to go back through the chapter if you are not sure.

Key points

There are key point boxes throughout the book. These sections draw your attention to important facts and definitions.

Margin comments

Margin comments contain advice and guidance and are separated from the main text because of their importance.

Practice questions

At the end of each chapter there are multiple-choice practice test questions to give you an idea of the type of questions you might be asked in your SATs exams. Test yourself to see how you're doing. The answers are on page 124.

1 Using data

1.1 Creating impact

What is impact?

When looking at this page, what stands out the most? Your eyes are drawn immediately to the picture. Your brain might automatically think, 'What's this about?' or 'Am I interested?'.

Straightaway, your attention has been grabbed and you want to know more. This is what creating impact is all about.

A successful poster will use images and colour to really catch the eye.

Which of these two posters would be more successful in attracting people to a school disco?

Disco

Saturday 24th August

Rob's Disco

at the Burnwell Centre

8:30 'til late

Ask yourself why the second poster stands out more. Can you think of three reasons?

Key Point   When producing a document, always think about the impact you want to create. Will your work stand out from others?

Try different colours and fonts to see if they improve the look.

You can create impact by your use of:
- images – adding graphics or a picture
- different fonts – emphasising a title or creating a style
- colour – different colours have different effects, and some colours work better together than others
- size of font – emphasising different parts of the text, e.g. titles and subtitles.
- the layout of the page – the eye is either drawn to the largest object on the page or just above the centre of the page.

1.2 Identifying purpose

Why are you producing this document?

When creating any document you need to be aware of what you are trying to achieve. Are you trying to publicise an event, advertise a product, present facts or opinions, or just entertain? Next time you watch television, notice how companies advertise cars. How are they persuading you to buy their car? Normally, they try to make you feel like you need the product to look good or to live a better life.

In the same way, paper documents have different purposes. Documents for different purposes are laid out in different ways. Look at the two documents below: one is a menu for a high-class restaurant, the other is an advert from the internet for children's toys.

STARTERS

Marinated salmon tartare, anchovy mayonnaise, poached quail's egg topped with caviar

Croustade of white crab meat, leaves salad and beetroot juice reduction

Raviole of goat cheese with basil and red pepper juice

Salmon terrine and pétoncles with artichokes and green asparagus salad

Apple and andouille tart fine with foie gras and Pommeau dressing

Starter of the day

MAIN COURSES

Rumsteck on marrow bone, confits vegetables, Madera sauce

Roast filet of pollock, rösti of potatoes, spiced spinach and red butter sauce

Entrecôte of veal poêlée, sweet potatoes purée, fricassée of mushrooms and two sauces

Fillet of pikeperch, courgettes with herbs, marmalade of cherry tomatoes with basil

Duck breast with pomme fondante, honey onion Tatin, cider sauce

Pig's trotter stuffed with black pudding with cumin and with celeriac purée
(Pied de cochon d'aujourd'hui suivant mon humeur)

> Look at examples of different layouts in magazines. Which ones are more successful?

The first document does not need to catch the eye, but needs to clearly inform the user about the choices on the menu. It also tries to convey a subtle message about the restaurant and its image. The second example is designed to advertise something, so uses bright colours, pictures and other means to catch the eye.

Think about what you would include on a poster to advertise a school sports day. Would you use colour, large pictures and large bold text? You need to consider whether the poster will be printed in black and white or colour, and where it will be placed.

Looking at newspapers

Look at the front page of a tabloid newspaper. How does it grab your attention – through size of headline, use of photographs, use of colour and graphics? The front page is designed to sell the paper, as well as communicate a story or put across an opinion. Now compare it with the front page of a broadsheet. What differences do you notice in the way the information is presented?

Key Points

When reading a document, you need to be aware of what the author is trying to achieve.

When producing a document, try to think about the best ways to achieve your aim.

Consider the different ways of laying out a document. Will it be a poster, a notice or a leaflet, or some other kind of document?

Decide whether the final document would be better in black and white or in colour.

1.3 Target audience

Who do you want to read the document?

> Remember the unwritten rule: the more text, the more adult the audience.

When producing a document you should always think about who will read it and why. You must remember that different age groups have different reading skills. Younger children will require shorter words and less complex language, while adults can cope with a wider vocabulary. Very old people might require larger text, but colour might be less important.

Here is an example of where using the right language for a particular audience makes understanding much easier.

Before progressing on to the penultimate stage of construction, one must ensure that the abutments are vertical and approach access has consolidated.

You must check that the bridge base is straight and the road has settled.

Another consideration is how much of the page is taken up by text and how much by images. For example, a child's reading book may be mostly pictures, whereas a novel may be completely text. Why do you think this is?

Key Points

- Understand the importance of size of text.

- Know that the language used (choice of words) really affects the reader's understanding.

- Be aware of the picture-to-text ratio on each page. Younger children will need more pictures to hold their interest.

1.4 Reliability and bias

Can you trust everything you read?

Not everything that you read is a fact. Many newspapers use their writer's opinions to sell a story. These opinions only give one viewpoint. You need to be clear of the difference between fact and opinion.

John is 12. He is a good boy.

Don't believe everything you read – sometimes opinions are portrayed as fact.

This statement contains a fact and an opinion. The fact cannot be denied – John is capable of proving beyond all doubt that he is 12 years old. Saying that he is good is only an opinion – he may only be good in his mother's eyes or in certain company, he may be good at football but bad at cricket.

Can you rely on this website to be accurate?

When looking at websites on the Internet, you need to take this into consideration. There are many sites produced by individuals that contain no facts and only give the author's opinion. Official sites, such as official fan club sites for pop stars or football teams, are often the best sources of factual information. But even these will portray their subject matter in a positive light.

Key Points

- Know the difference between fact and opinion, and be able to spot this in documents.

- Be aware of bias in different kinds of media.

- Consider whether a website is biased or not.

- Look at different sources if you want to produce a balanced argument.

In some websites the author wants to try to convince you that their opinion is correct. They will give all the arguments for one side of the story and conveniently ignore all the opposition's arguments. This is often true for topical and political discussions. For example, if you look at websites about fox hunting, you will see some that are against it, and some that are for it. The best sites to find are those that can see both sides of the argument, that are more objective and less biased.

Skills Check

- Do you know how to use WordArt?
- Can you copy and paste images?
- Can you create text boxes?

Progress Check

1. What should you think about when making an advert?
2. How would a page designed for a child differ from one designed for an adult?
3. When looking at a website about a topical issue, why should you check who has produced it?

1. Colourful, large lettering, image, audience. 2. Less text, larger picture, bigger writing on child's page. 3. They might be presenting a one-sided viewpoint, opinion rather than fact.

Practice questions

1 You have been asked to design an invitation to your little brother's birthday party. What must you consider before you actually start your design? Your brother is five.

....

....

.... **[3 marks]**

2

List five ways that you could improve this poster to make it more likely to attract the interest of 15 year olds.

....

....

....

....

.... **[5 marks]**

3 **(a)** You have been asked to find out the tour dates for the Red Hot Chilli Peppers. You find three sites on the Internet all with different dates. How is this possible?

....

.... **[1 mark]**

(b) List three clues that there might be to find out which site has the correct dates?

....

....

....

.... **[3 marks]**

4 In speeches, politicians might choose to present as facts details that are their opinions. Why might they do this?

....

....

.... **[2 marks]**

5 Give two factors that might affect the ability of an audience to understand a document.

....

....

.... **[2 marks]**

Multiple choice questions

1   What is the most effective way of grabbing initial attention on a magazine cover?

    a   Long words.
    b   Big colourful picture.
    c   WordArt with a shadow.
    d   Lots of white space.

2   In a big hall there are lots of people giving presentations.
    What tactic would make yours stand out more than the others?

    a   Black text on a white background.
    b   Lots of slides changing quickly.
    c   A sudden relevant noise.
    d   Colourful background and text.

3   What is the best way to ensure that information you find on the
    Internet is reliable?

    a   Only use one search engine.
    b   Choose the top hit from the search list.
    c   Only look at official websites.
    d   Only look at URLs ending *.com*

4   Large black and white text, few pictures and complex language would
    suit which audience best?

    a   Elderly people.
    b   Young children.
    c   Teenagers.
    d   Professional business people.

5   If you are inviting someone to a party, what kind of writing would be most appropriate?

    a   Persuasive.
    b   Educational.
    c   Informative.
    d   Argumentative.

2 Searching and selecting

After studying this topic you should be able to:

- identify where to find information
- search for and find relevant facts, data and information
- set up advanced searches
- reference work
- spot patterns in data
- check your work to make sure it is suitable.

2.1 Identifying sources and basic searching

There are many places to look for information. Traditionally, the best place to go for information was a library. This is still sometimes the case. However, there are now lots more places where you can find more up-to-date information electronically, such as the Internet or Teletext.

The type of information you need and what you want to do with it will dictate where you look for it. Sometimes, printed reference books are the best choice. They would be preferable when you want to be sure about the source of the information – you can actually see where the information comes from and who wrote it. An example of this would be using an atlas to find the state religion of a country – if you looked on the Internet for this, it would be difficult to find and might be influenced by the opinion of the writer.

If you are looking for very up-to-date information, Teletext or the Internet would be better. For, while a printed book might have been published several years previously, information on Teletext or the Internet is constantly being updated. However, you should realise that information on websites can be out-of-date too. If you want to use the information you have found and adapt it, it would be helpful to use the Internet, as text can be copied and pasted into an application such as Microsoft Word™.

So long as you bear in mind that the information on websites can be posted by anybody, so might not be correct, and you remember to check that the information is not out-of-date, then searching the Internet might be a good option.

> If you are searching for a fact and have access to reference books, this will probably be a quicker way of finding the information.

Once you have decided that you are going to use the Internet to find the information, you need to think about how you will carry out your search. You may already know the address of the site, in which case, just type it into the address bar. Normally, you will not know the website you need, in which case you need to use a search engine or a directory.

Directories will find fewer websites than search engines will, but often better ones.

The difference between these is that a search engine will search for key words on websites, while a directory will have categories that you can select by clicking on the links. The links on a directory have been selected and checked by people employed by the company to make sure they are appropriate.

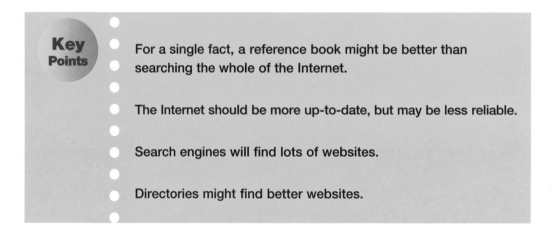

Key Points

- For a single fact, a reference book might be better than searching the whole of the Internet.

- The Internet should be more up-to-date, but may be less reliable.

- Search engines will find lots of websites.

- Directories might find better websites.

2.2 Referencing your work

Authors find information from many different places, and usually include references to show the source of this information. This is done for two main reasons: first to acknowledge work that is not their own because this is required by the Copyright, Patents and Design Act 1989. Second, it reminds the author where they found the information, in case they want to elaborate the point, and it shows the reader where they can find out more.

It is good practice always to reference your work. There is a standard way of doing this, an example of which is:

Note that the title is written in italics.

Author/s, *title of book* (city of publication, publisher, date).

For example, to reference this book, you should write:

Max Begley & David Sadler, *Revise KS3 ICT* (London, Letts Educational, 2004).

Now we have discussed what a reference is, we can look at how to reference information within a document. If you have included a picture downloaded from the Internet you can include a caption with the image (e.g. *ref 1*) and at the end of the document state the address (URL) of the website and the photographer's name, if you have it, next to the reference number.

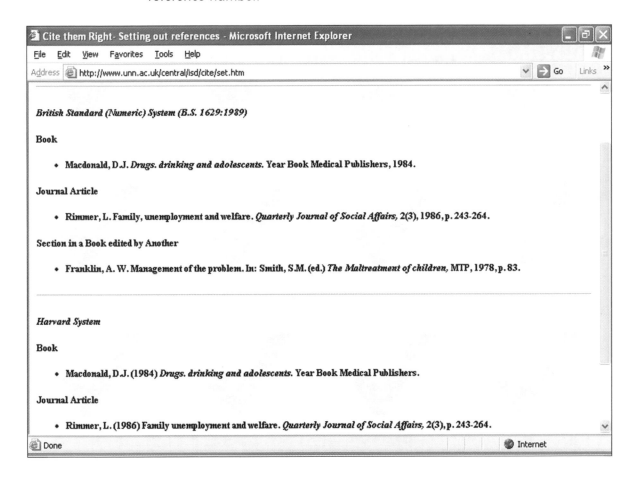

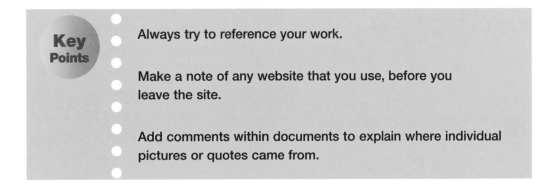

Key Points

Always try to reference your work.

Make a note of any website that you use, before you leave the site.

Add comments within documents to explain where individual pictures or quotes came from.

2.3 Advanced searches

If you search the Internet using a search engine, you will probably find lots of websites. Rather than visiting each one to see which is best, there are different methods of refining the search.

For example, if you typed *cheese* into a search engine, you would come up with thousands of websites. The easiest way of refining your search is to use more than one word and put a plus sign in between, e.g. *cheddar+cheese*, so that the search engine will look for sites with both words. This can be made even more specific by using speech marks, e.g. *"Cheddar cheese"*. If you do this the search engine will search for these two words in this order with nothing in between them. You can reduce the number of sites found by including a minus sign, e.g. *"Cheddar cheese"-caves*, so that any sites with the word 'caves' are not included in your results.

> You can use words like *AND*, *NOT* and *OR* instead of symbols.

The second method is to search within results. This will search only the sites already found for a second keyword.

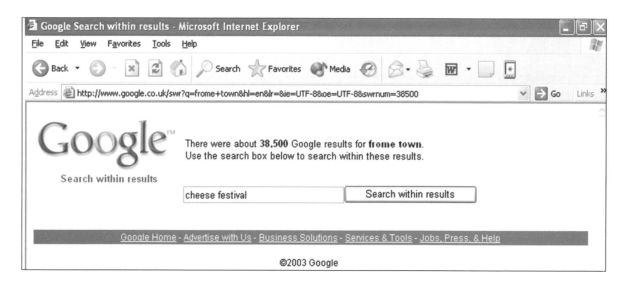

Using these symbols or words to search is called using Boolean operators. There are other terms that can be used when searching:

> When searching for names, always use speech marks and capital letters.

near – This means that websites with the keywords near each other will be in the results.

wild card – If you are not sure of the spelling or only know part of the word, you can use what is called a wildcard. This is an asterisk that replaces unknown letters, e.g. *arch*ology* should find sites about archaeology.

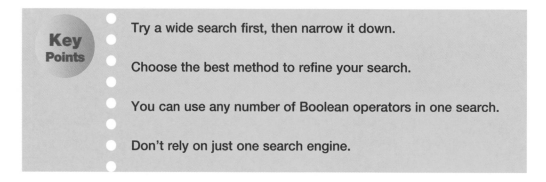

Key Points

- Try a wide search first, then narrow it down.
- Choose the best method to refine your search.
- You can use any number of Boolean operators in one search.
- Don't rely on just one search engine.

2.4 Patterns in data

There are many different ways of displaying data. Some are easier to interpret than others, e.g. a long list of numbers in a table is more difficult to understand than a graph of the same data. By displaying information in a graph you help the reader to see any patterns immediately.

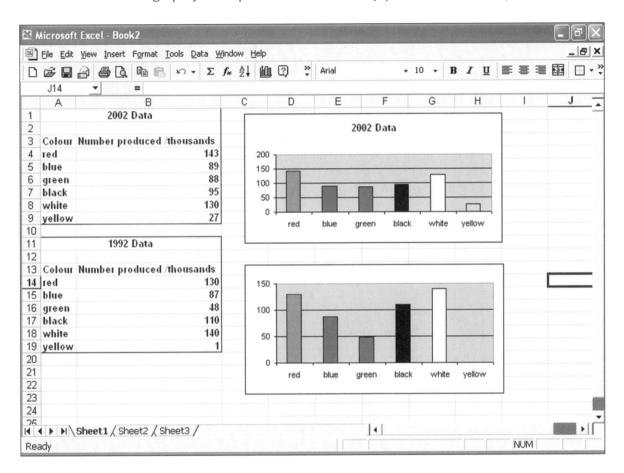

> Make sure that the graph you have chosen displays the information in the clearest way possible.

The information shown above is the same but in two different forms. You can quickly see which car colour is most popular at any one time on the graph.

There are four main types of graph you would use at Key Stage 3: bar chart, scatter graph, line graph and pie chart. Examples of the four types can be found on the next page.

Once you have chosen the type of graph, you then need to decide the scale that you are going to use. This must be relevant to the subject – for example, if you have a very small scale, a tiny difference in results can look very significant, when actually it is unimportant.

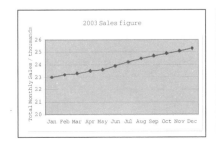
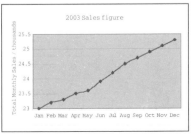

Which of the two sales charts on the previous page implies the biggest growth? Look at the numbers and find out who has actually sold more.

Type of graph	When used	Example
Bar chart	This is a set of bars or columns of equal width. It is used for discrete data (separate pieces) or continuous data. The height of the bar shows the frequency.	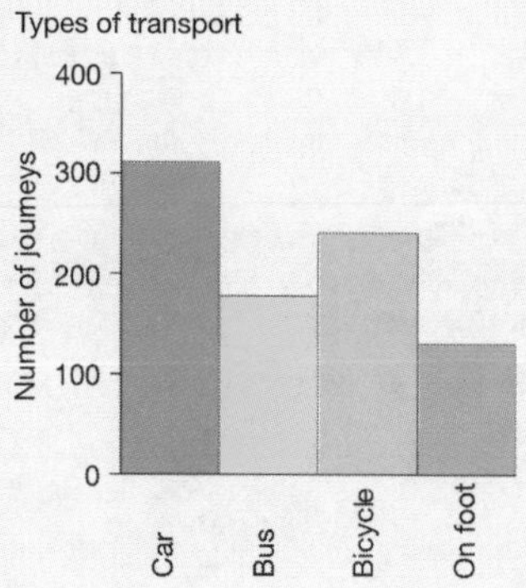
Scatter graph	This is used to show whether two sets of data are related. The graph shows the correlation (connection) between the data.	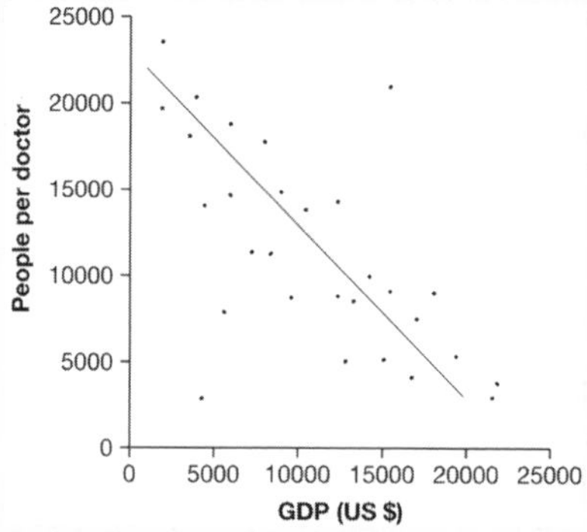
Line graph	This consists of points joined by lines. It can be used to show continuous data and how a quantity changes over time.	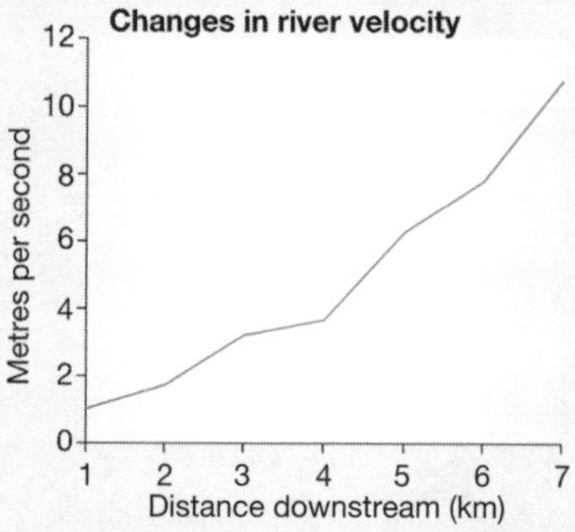
Pie chart	A pie chart is a circle split into sections to show the percentage or share of different items.	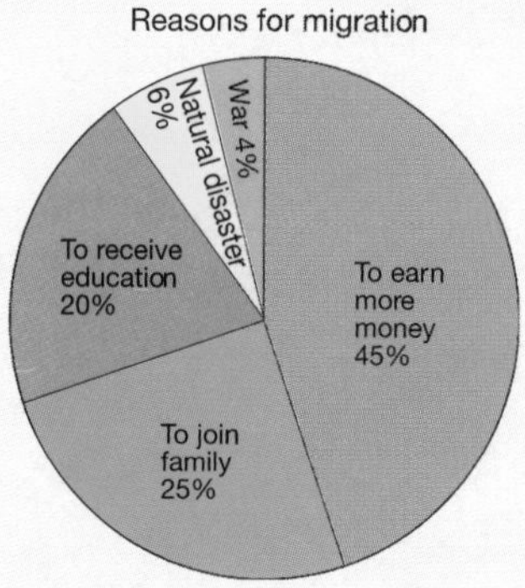

Key Points

Ensure that all graphs have a title, labelled axes and a scale and that they are clear to read.

Choose your graph carefully – try different options and use the most appropriate.

Think about what you are trying to achieve with the chart – do you want a big scale to emphasise a point?

2.5 Verifying your work

Everybody makes mistakes. It is therefore important that you always check that anything you have typed is correct. This can be done in three ways:

- automated spellchecking
- proofreading
- making the computer read the work back to you.

Spellchecking

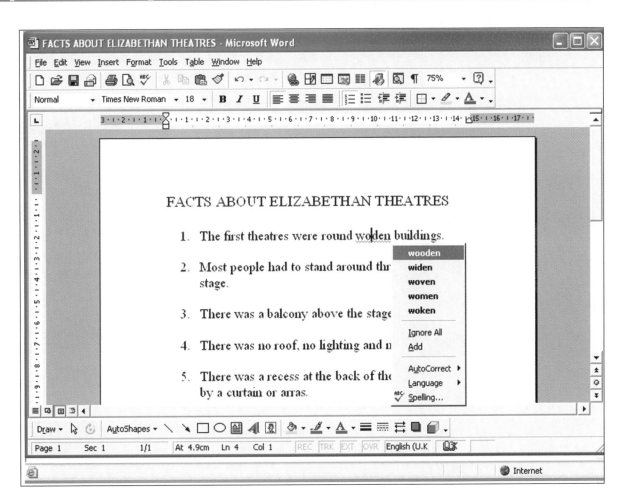

You need to be careful that the dictionary on the computer is set to the correct language – if it is set up for English (US), then *centre* and *colour*, for example, will be spelled the American way – *center* and *color*.

Spellchecking is the first step in verifying your work. The computer has an in-built dictionary and it compares the words you write with words in it. This does not mean that any highlighted word is necessarily misspelled, or that any verified word is necessarily the correct word. The problem is that the computer does not know what you are trying to say.

The following sentence would *not* be highlighted by a spellchecker:

Tonight's mane event starts at 7 o'clock.

The word *mane* is the wrong spelling of the word, but it is still a word.

An example of a correct sentence that would be highlighted is:

Amery Hill School and Frogmore Community College play football next Wednesday evening.

The names of the schools are not in the standard in-built dictionary.

Proofreading

You can also use grammar check (underlined in green) to make sure you are using correct English. However, these are limited in their usefulness.

Proofreading is reading through your work afterwards to check that it makes sense and there are no grammatical or typing errors. It is often better to have somebody else proofread your work because you tend to read the word as you thought it when you were writing it, not as it actually appears.

This is so important that some people do it for a job. Every book published will have been read by an editor, whose job it is to make sure that there are no errors.

Key Points

- Make sure the dictionary is set up correctly.

- Don't assume the computer is always write (right!).

- Get a friend to proofread your work.

- Find out if your computer can read your work back to you.

- If you don't know how to spell a word, have a go, the spellchecker may be able to give you the correct version.

Text to voice applications

Some computer applications are able to read your work back to you aloud. This means that you can listen to the computer as you read your original notes. This tool is very useful for people who are partially sighted, dyslexics and people who have difficulty with spelling.

Skills Check

- Can you use advanced Internet searches?
- Do you know how to reference your work?
- Can you create and label a suitable graph correctly?
- Can you use a spellchecker correctly?

Progress Check

1 How can you get fewer hits when searching for a website?
2 When referencing work, which words should be in italics?
3 When should you use a pie chart to show data?

1. Use a more specific phrase in speech marks, add more keywords connected with *AND* (or use other Boolean operators), search within the results. 2. The title of the book. 3. To show percentages or proportions.

Practice questions

1 Why might you find information or a website on one search engine but not on another?

....

....

.... **[1 mark]**

2 Explain why it is very important to reference your work.

....

....

.... **[1 mark]**

3 What techniques might someone use to distort information when presenting it as a graph?

....

....

....

....

....

....

.... **[3 marks]**

Multiple choice questions

1 An example of verification is:

   a Copying your friend's work.
   b Proofreading your friend's work.
   c Asking the teacher whether your work is correct.
   d Printing your work.

2 What must you always include when referencing your work?

   a Title, author, publisher.
   b Title, author, publisher, date, age.
   c Title, author, publisher, date.
   d Title, author, publisher, date, genre, medium.

3 An example of a Boolean operator is:

   a RED
   b AND
   c OF COURSE
   d NOW

4 Which of the following is **not** a common symbol used when searching the Internet?

   a +
   b "
   c ^
   d –

5 A good way of reducing the number of irrelevant websites found by a search engine is by:

   a Adding more key words.
   b Only looking at the first page in the search list.
   c Reducing the number of keywords.
   d Adding the word 'OR' between key words.

3 Organising and investigating

3.1   Using databases

A database is a collection of information which can be broken down into component parts to enable it to be searched. A good example of this is the *Yellow Pages*. If you wanted to search for a garage, you could look for garages in your local area. If you then looked more closely, you would be able to find the garages nearest to you.

There are a few key phrases that are essential to understand when using databases:

Data	Numbers or letters that could mean anything by themselves.
Information	Numbers or letters that have been put in context so that they inform you about something.
Record	A collection of data about an individual person or object.
Field	A group of similar data, e.g. age or first name.
Field name	The label given to a field.
Field size	The maximum number of characters that can be used in a field.
Field type	The type of data expected to be entered into the field, e.g. text or numbers.
Filter	Show only the relevant information.
Search	Try to find records with specific data.
Sort	Arrange all records in a specified order, e.g. alphabetically, chronologically or numerically.

When you use a database, it will usually be in form view. This is designed for ease of entering information, so that anyone can use it. Only one field can be selected at a time and only one record can be seen at a time. Another benefit of using forms is user confidentiality, which means that when a user is inserting their data, they cannot see information about others. This is important when addresses, telephone numbers and other personal information are included.

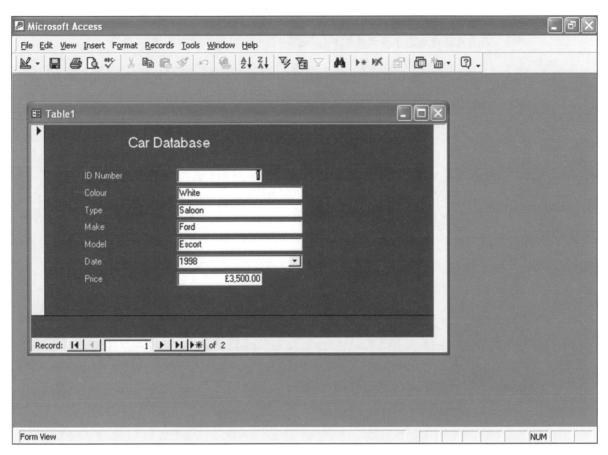

Sometimes you will need to print out information from a database. When you do this, you should be in report view. This is the easiest way to print out the required data. You normally select the necessary information before the report is produced. An example of a report might be the number of people who have yet to pay an invoice. It would include their name, address, telephone number and how much they have left to pay.

Forms are on-screen data capture forms. They have the same function as a questionnaire but can look more professional. The main advantage is that the data can be analysed electronically.

Key Points

- A database is made up of data which then becomes information when you add a label to give it meaning.

- Data is generally entered on to a database in 'form' view.

- A whole database is very rarely printed out.

3.2 Designing and creating databases

When designing a database the most important questions to ask are: What information do you need? For what purpose are you going to use the database? You need to do this for three reasons: first, so that you collect the relevant data; second, so that you follow the rules of the Data Protection Act 1998; and finally, so that you don't waste time and disk space collecting and storing irrelevant information.

Once you have chosen the information, you need to decide what names to give the fields and what size they need to be. The best way to do this is to design the 'form' view of the database by hand on paper.

Some people would choose to plan the database in more detail by drawing out a table like the one below:

Field name	Field size	Field type	Validation	Notes
Title	4	Text	Mr/Mrs/Miss/Ms/Dr/Prof etc.	
First name	15	Text		
Surname	30	Text		
Date of birth	10	Date	Range check >18 and <65	DD/MM/YYYY
Account no.	8	Number	Number only, must be entered	Must be exactly 8 characters

Spending time planning at this stage can save a lot of time later on; there is nothing worse than having to redraft everything because you have missed out a vital field.

Decide on what forms to use, what will need printing out and what searches (queries) are needed. It is always a good idea to hand-draw this quickly on paper first, just so that you know what you want to produce. The form will be on screen most often, so this needs to look really good – appropriate for the end user and for the task that it is designed for.

> Whenever you can, use lookup wizards, as these reduce the amount of errors.

Lookup wizards can be used to give the user a limited number of optional answers, such as gender (male/female) or age (11/12/13/14/15/16). This means that the user cannot enter invalid data into the field.

A query will not be seen by the end user, so how it looks is irrelevant. Queries need to be set up for each possible search needed. An example of a query is shown below:

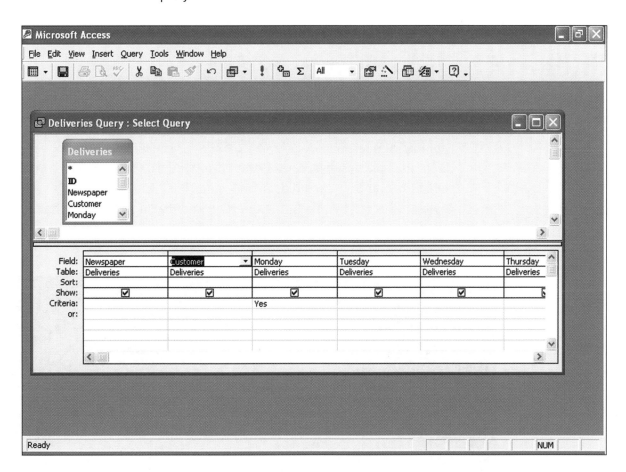

The query above will search for customers who have papers delivered on a Monday.

Anything printed out from a database should be in report form. Therefore, when creating a database, you should think of all the queries that you may want to print out, and link a report to them.

Once your database is finished, you should check that everything works. The best way to do this is by using a test example. Think of questions to search the database with and all the jobs that will be done with the database and use examples to make sure that they work.

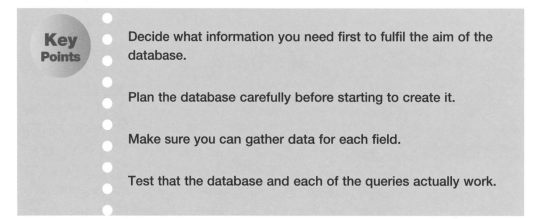

Key Points

- Decide what information you need first to fulfil the aim of the database.

- Plan the database carefully before starting to create it.

- Make sure you can gather data for each field.

- Test that the database and each of the queries actually work.

3.3   Collecting data

There are three ways of collecting data on paper. First, there is an individual questionnaire. This is a form that is filled in by one person answering a number of questions. A data capture form is similar to a questionnaire, but is for multiple answers. This is often displayed as a table with column headings and each record as an individual line. Finally, on a tally sheet, data is collected by asking the question and making a mark to indicate how many people choose a selected answer.

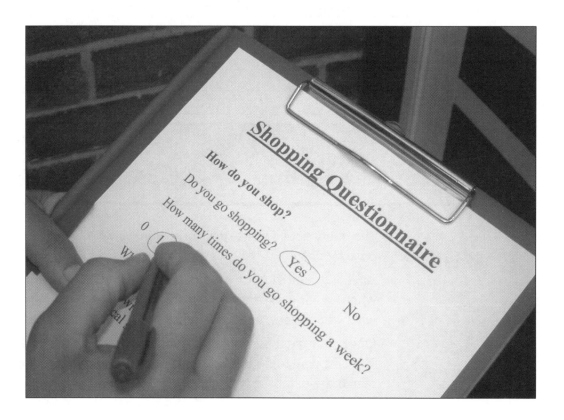

	A	B	C	D	E	F
1	Membership Number	Name	Surname	DOB	Date joined	Paid 2003
2	100013453	Max	Begley	14/07/1969	01/06/1990	n
3	100013454	Dave	Sadler	13/06/1971	01/06/1990	y
4	100013455	Karen	Krajewska	14/03/1965	01/06/1990	y
5	100013456	Andy	Vowell	03/03/1959	01/06/1990	y
6	100013457	Karen	Mattick	10/12/1982	01/06/1990	y
7	100013458	Mark	Palmer	13/08/1993	01/06/1990	y
8	100013459	Murray	Thompson	12/04/1986	01/08/1991	y
9	100013460	Rachel	Sadler	01/01/1976	01/08/1991	y
10	100013461	Ahmed	Ali	17/09/1972	01/08/1991	y
11	100013462	Deesh	Grewal	18/02/1989	01/08/1991	n
12	100013463	Malcolm	Dickson	13/05/1976	01/09/1991	n
13	100013464	Gideon	Williams	02/05/1974	01/11/1993	y
14	100013465	Nilam	Patel	13/10/1963	01/11/1993	y
15	100013466	Shairoz	Wilson	14/08/1958	01/03/1995	y
16	100013467	Jason	Waring	12/07/1958	01/03/1995	y
17	100013468	Sarah	Hayward	13/11/1973	01/06/1996	n

Colour of Cars

Red   ‖‖‖ ‖‖

Blue   ‖‖‖ ‖‖

Green   ‖‖‖‖

Black   ‖‖‖

White   ‖‖‖ ‖

You must be sure that you are aware of all the issues in the Data Protection Act 1998 before collecting data.

It is important to understand when you would use each method of collecting data. Obviously if you are using a database and can have your computer with you, you can enter the information directly on to the form on the database. When you are collecting personal information, the law says that you should keep an individual's data private. This means you cannot use a tally sheet or a data capture form as the information from many sources is on one sheet.

Questionnaires use a lot of paper, so whenever possible you should use a data capture form or tally sheet, if you cannot use a computer. The choice is dependent on the type of question you are asking. If the answers are limited to yes/no, or there is a limited choice of answers, then a tally sheet works equally well.

3.4 Validation

When you type anything into a computer, you should always check that it is correct before moving on. This is called verification. In many applications, the computer can help you with this – a good example is spellcheck, which underlines any words in your document that do not appear in the computer's dictionary. You could also do this by reading through your work – this is called manual verification or proofreading.

Validation is a completely different way of checking information, which is done by the computer. As you type in information, the computer checks that what you have entered is what it expects. For example, if you answer the question, 'How old are you?' with the answer 'purple', a validation check will realise that this is not a number so it will produce an error message 'Answer not valid', which usually appears as a pop-up menu on the screen.

> Do not confuse verification and validation.
> Validation has a 'd' as has 'data entry', while verification has a 'c', as has 'checking'.

There are a number of types of validation:

Drop-down menu	A limited range of answers where the operator selects from a list
Data type	The computer only allows the specified data as an answer.
Range check	The answer must be within a specified range of numbers.
Answer required	The operator must answer this question.
Field size	The operator cannot type in too many or too few characters.

3.5 Drawing graphs

When drawing a graph, do not forget to select your graph type carefully (see topic 2.4 for more information). Drawing graphs is much easier on a computer than by hand. It is easier to produce, edit and label a graph using a chart wizard. It is not always better to produce a graph on a computer, as for some tasks, it is easier to read a hand-drawn graph.

The control key can be used for many things – selecting more than one item is the most common. It can be used for this in almost any application.

If you select the information for a graph correctly before starting the wizard it will make life easier. If you are using Microsoft Excel™ and the columns of information are next to each other, this is easy as all you need to do is select them. If the columns are not next to each other, you will need to select each column individually, holding down the control key (Ctrl) to keep the previous selection.

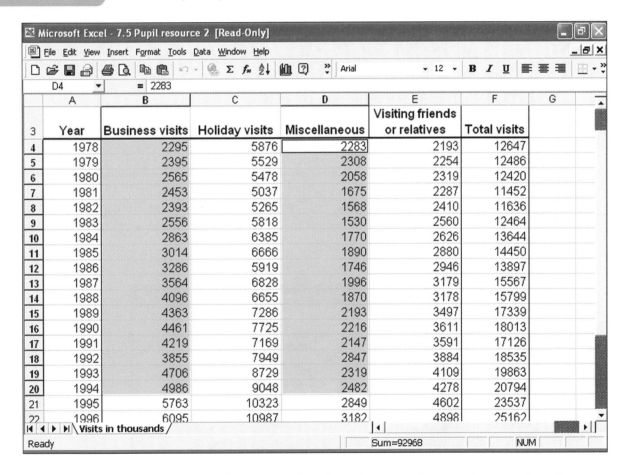

The most common mistake when drawing a line graph is to select 'line graph' in the chart wizard. This will plot each column as a separate line, not one versus the other. If you need one column as the x axis, and the other as the y axis, then you need to use 'scatter graph'.

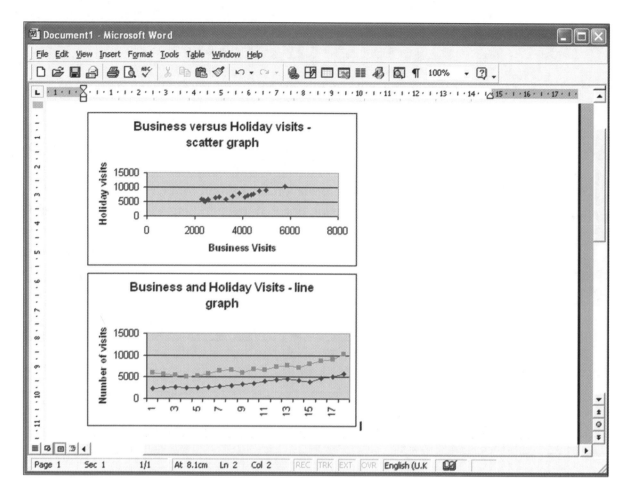

You can check that you have selected the information correctly before getting too far through the chart wizard by clicking on the 'Press and hold to view sample' button.

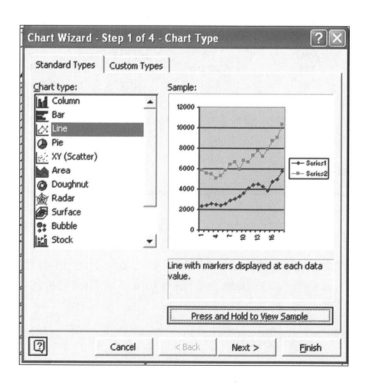

If you have not selected the information correctly, you can either start the wizard again with the new selection, or you can go on to the second screen on the chart wizard. When you click on 'series', you can select the information using the icon next to the cell range.

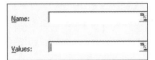

Once you have selected the correct information, you can then carry on with the chart wizard. Labels and titles for the axes can be added later in the wizard or after you have finished. Colours can be changed by double clicking on that line or section after finishing the wizard.

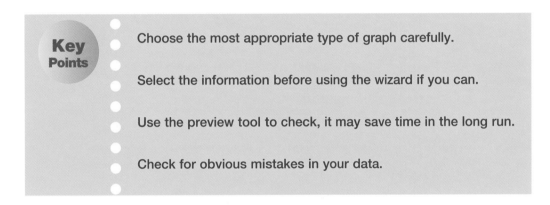

Key Points

- Choose the most appropriate type of graph carefully.

- Select the information before using the wizard if you can.

- Use the preview tool to check, it may save time in the long run.

- Check for obvious mistakes in your data.

3.6 Using formulae

A formula is a calculation that the computer carries out automatically. It is used so that the computer does the calculating rather than you, e.g. in a spreadsheet. This means that difficult calculations can be performed repeatedly without the operator typing in lots of information. Formulae can also easily be copied.

But I could have done that anyway.

It can be helpful to use formulae even for very simple calculations, as they speed up the calculations, and if you need to change one of the numbers, the formula will automatically be re-calculated and the new answer displayed.

To understand formulae, you need to understand the terms **rule** and **variable**. **Variables** are the numbers that are put into the formula. If you have 4 tickets that cost £5 each, the variables are 4 and 5. It is possible that the tickets might have been more expensive, or we might have needed more – these numbers may change, so are called variables. The total cost will always equal the number of tickets multiplied by the price. This never changes, no matter what the variables are – this is a **rule**.

> A rule is determined by a formula. Whatever the variables, the relationship will not change.

In a spreadsheet, the computer knows that you are typing in a formula if you start the sum with an equals sign (=). Here are some examples of a few basic formulae:

=A2+300	Whatever is in cell A2 add 300.
=SUM(A2:A5)	Cells A2, A3, A4, A5 added together
=A2*A3	Whatever is in cell A2 multiplied by the contents of cell A3

If you want to use more complex formulae, you can use **brackets**, e.g. =(A2/57)*100 might be the formula to work out a percentage where cell A2 contains the score out of 57. For very advanced formulae, you can use the **function wizard**.

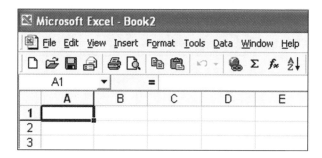

This lets you select the function you need and will explain to you what number to write where. The screen shots below show you how to use a function wizard to calculate the rank order of a set of data.

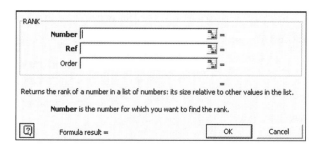

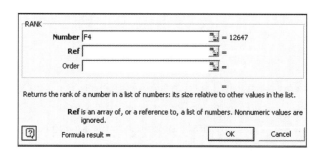

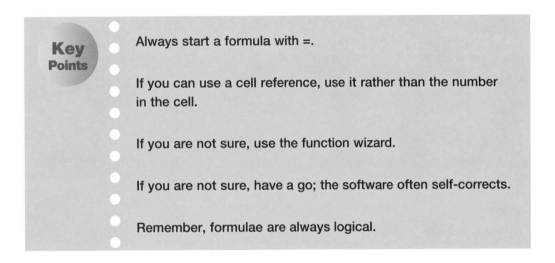

Always start a formula with =.

If you can use a cell reference, use it rather than the number in the cell.

If you are not sure, use the function wizard.

If you are not sure, have a go; the software often self-corrects.

Remember, formulae are always logical.

3.7 Finding relationships and patterns

The best way to see a trend in a scattergraph is to draw a best fit line. This is a straight line or a curve that goes through or near to as many of the points as possible. It is designed to eliminate any anomalous results (results that don't fit the pattern) that might have been recorded.

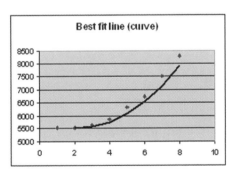

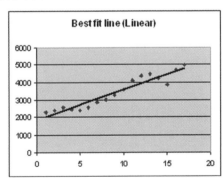

It is sometimes easier to observe a pattern or the optimum result if you use graphs in combination with formulae, rather than looking at the data in numerical form.

By looking at the graph you should be able to come to a conclusion. There are four types of information you can get from a scatter graph. You will either need to look at the intercept (where the line crosses the vertical axis), the gradient (the slope of the line) or the area underneath the line. The fourth type of information is where the line is extended to estimate the value at a point higher or lower than those recorded.

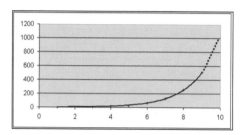

On a pie chart you are generally looking at percentages or proportions, and on a bar chart only the values recorded are important. A histogram is like a bar chart but the difference is that the area under all the columns is important too.

> **Key Points**
> - Decide if the pattern in your information is better seen as a graph.
> - Label best fit lines appropriately.
> - Don't be afraid to start the wizard again and choose a different type of graph.

3.8 Drawing conclusions

When drawing a conclusion (in scientific projects) you should explain what you have proved. The conclusion should be related to the aim of the task and compared to the hypothesis (if one has been made). If you have made predictions you should comment on their accuracy – it is not a bad thing to have made a prediction which is different from your results, as you can often get more marks by explaining why there is a difference.

> Remember, a conclusion is about the result and not how you got it.

You should always comment on how reliable your results were and how you could improve the tests or experiment. Some improvements that normally can be applied are:

- change the range of results taken to focus on one small part of the original range
- widen the range
- change the scale on the axes
- use more precise measuring equipment
- repeat results to make them more reliable.

> Comment on how fair the test was. Were the conditions the same for each test?

> **Key Points**
> A conclusion should include:
> - comments relating to the aim
> - a brief description of results
> - comparison of prediction and hypothesis to the result
> - any improvements that could be made.

3.9 Databases in society

Databases are one of the main uses of IT. In retailing they are used to keep track of who is buying what and when. Most of the larger stores now have a reward card scheme that helps to gather precise information about who buys what. Shops also use databases for stock control. They use an Electronic Point Of Sale (EPOS) system to keep track of what is leaving the shop, which helps them decide when to order more goods. Stock is identified by a Unique Product Code (UPC) for each individual item. This is scanned using a bar code reader.

> Databases can hold massive amounts of information, which can be searched very quickly.

Banks also use databases to store information on each account. The information is kept in a central database so it can be accessed from anywhere in the world, with the correct password. Some of the larger databases keep track of spending on credit cards – any transaction by any credit card is noted.

Databases have also helped in the public sector: police can keep central records that can be accessed from any police station; hospitals can call up records centrally in case you fall ill away from home; census information is collected every ten years and can be stored on a database, taking up a lot less space than the Domesday Book and making it far easier to search.

Small industries can benefit by using databases, e.g. car showrooms can now search each others' databases for cars or parts to try to satisfy the customer as quickly as possible. They can also keep better track of what is in their showroom or stock cupboard. (See next page for an example of this use of databases by small businesses.)

Some companies use databases for their own benefit even though they weren't designed for them. One example of this is the use of email. Marketing companies can obtain lists of people in certain categories and contact them with relevant offers via 'junk' email. Some companies send junk mail to as many email addresses as they can, just in case they find a buyer. This is called spam.

Sending junk mail is not really abusing databases, although it can be irritating. But some databases could be abused if the Data Protection Act (DPA) is not properly adhered to. The main points of the DPA are:

- information needs to be obtained legally
- it should only be collected if relevant

- it must be kept up-to-date
- it should be accessible to the person the information is about
- it must be kept secure
- it can only be kept if still needed
- it cannot be used for any other purpose
- it cannot be transferred to any company in a country that does not adhere to the DPA.

The DPA was introduced in 1984 and revised in 1998 because of the increasing use of the Internet. The new act came into effect on 31 January 2000.

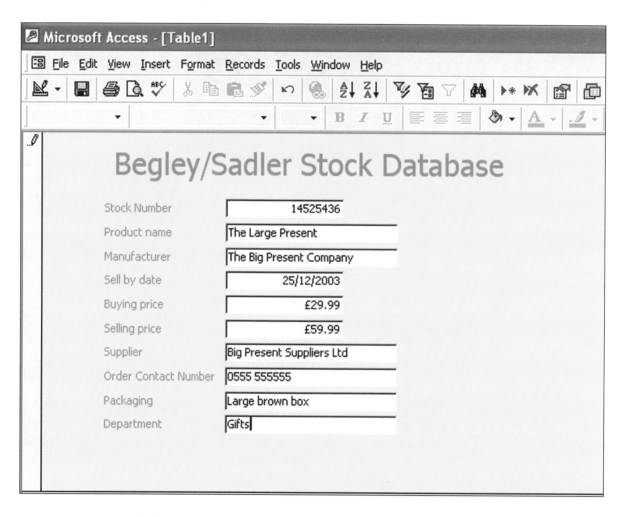

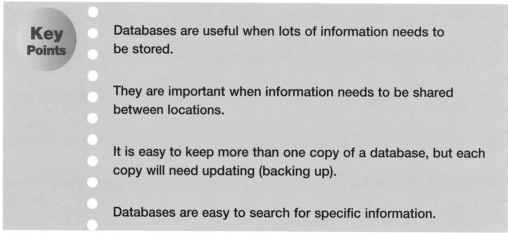

Key Points

Databases are useful when lots of information needs to be stored.

They are important when information needs to be shared between locations.

It is easy to keep more than one copy of a database, but each copy will need updating (backing up).

Databases are easy to search for specific information.

Skills Check

- Do you know the purpose of a form, report and query in a database?
- Do you know what a field and a record are?
- Are you aware when you should use a questionnaire rather than a tally sheet?
- Can you choose the correct field type for each field?
- Can you explain the difference between verification and validation?

Progress Check

1 What kind of graph would you draw if you had measured how the temperature of a cup of tea had changed over time? Why would you choose this kind of graph?

2 You have been asked to collect information about homeowners and their income. What would be the best way to collect this information? What other method of collecting information could you use in different circumstances?

3 What formula would you use to find out the largest number in a column from cells A1 to A45?

1. Scatter graph because you can add best fit lines, calculate the gradient and easily plot one against the other. 2. An anonymous questionnaire. A survey when the information you are collecting is not of a personal nature. 3. =MAX(A1:A45)

Practice questions

1 Give three advantages of storing data in a database rather than on paper.

....

....

....

....

.... **[3 marks]**

2 What factors do you need to take into account when collecting data?

....

....

....

.... **[3 marks]**

3 Give five advantages of using spreadsheets to perform calculations over a basic calculator.

....

....

....

....

....

.... **[5 marks]**

Multiple choice questions

1 Which one of the following statements is false?

   a Databases take up less space than filing cabinets.
   b Databases can be searched very quickly.
   c Databases are easier to use than photocopiers.
   d Databases can be moved more easily than paper records.

2 Which field would be the best choice for a key field?

   a Surname.
   b Gender.
   c Membership number.
   d Date of birth.

3 Which of the following fields could be set up with a Boolean operator?

   a Name.
   b Age.
   c Gender.
   d Date of birth.

4 What is the most sensible coding for a gender field in a database?

   a 1 and 0.
   b male and female.
   c M and F.
   d B and G.

5 Which is the correct formula to add up all the cells between B2 and B28?

   a SUM B2:B28
   b =SUM(B2,B28)
   c =SUM B2:B28
   d =SUM(B2:B28)

4 Analysing and automating processes

4.1 Using and creating templates

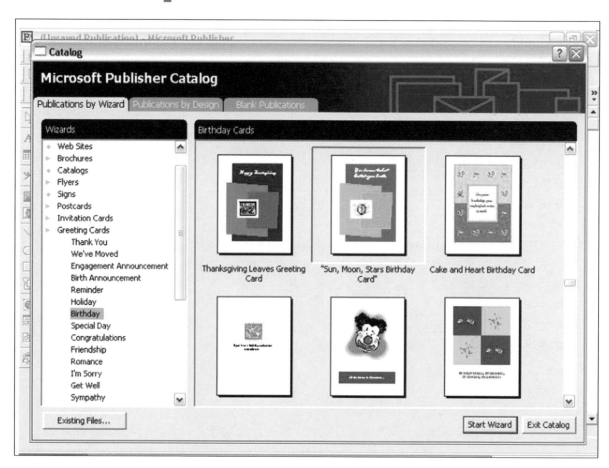

A **template** is a page or slide layout with no detail inserted. Some templates have examples placed to prompt a user where to input information. These are useful for documents where you want to have a consistent style or where the document is produced regularly. It is essential to use templates where different people need to produce similar documents. Good examples of this are found in Microsoft Publisher™, as they are in most desktop publishing packages – if you want to make a quick birthday card, you can choose a style from a selection of templates.

Sometimes no suitable template has been produced, so you will need to create one if you are going to be efficient. Templates can be made in any application and normally consist of boxes with text in. The template should include the design, i.e. the colour scheme to be used, font size, font type, positioning of text, size of image and can include suggested text. A template that might be used for the front cover of a magazine would certainly include all these things.

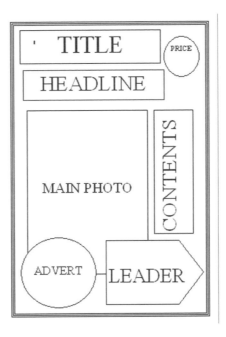

Remember, the template might need to be used by a beginner. It should be simple to adapt.

Templates are not only used for desktop publishing, they can be used for something as simple as a letter or as complex as a spreadsheet and graph or animated presentation. Templates in Excel are often called style sheets. The master slide in Microsoft PowerPoint™ automatically adds the colour scheme and background to any new slide.

Microsoft packages try to make their templates easier to use by having a 'wizard' that asks questions to help you adapt the template you have chosen.

Key Points

- Templates are used where there is a standard look to the document.

- They should be simple to use and adapt.

- Templates are often provided with applications to get you started.

- 'Wizards' often help by breaking the process of creating a template into small steps.

4.2 Understanding flowcharts

A flowchart is a drawing to represent a task or system broken down into a number of stages. The diagram shows each logical step in the system, each decision that needs to be made and the results of those decisions. Programmers use flowcharts to try to avoid bugs in the process. Flowcharts have different symbols to represent different parts of the process. There are different symbols for different kinds of flowcharts.

Program flowcharts

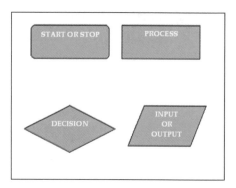

System flowcharts

You can buy software that is specifically designed to draw flowcharts.

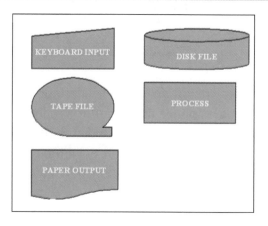

A process is a stage where something happens.

An input is when data or an item is put into a system.

An output is when something is displayed, printed or produced.

A decision is when there can be more than one outcome. Each outcome needs to lead to a process or stop box.

An example of a flowchart showing password checking during network logins is shown below.

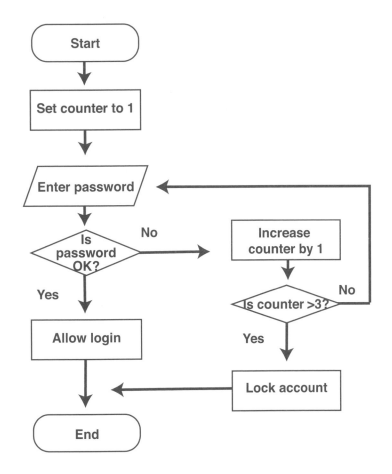

Key Points

- Flowcharts must always have a start and stop position but can include complete circles of flow.

- Flowcharts have specific shapes for different types of task.

- Flowcharts can help check that a system works before it is built or implemented.

4.3 Drawing design specification diagrams

A design specification diagram is a way to show as simply as possible what your system will do. It clearly shows the main stages of the system and how the information or resources flow through it. An example of a design specification diagram is shown in the *Water ride* case study in chapter 10 on page 118.

Keep this diagram simple, just include the main points.

Too much information on the diagram will make it harder to understand.

To implement the system all you need to do is to take one part of the diagram at a time, add the detail and make it work.

Key Points

- Keep the diagram simple, you can add detail later when you break it down into stages.

- Add pictures if you want to help explain.

4.4 Using macros

Any button on a toolbar is a **macro**. A macro is a series of tasks which have been automated so that the job can be done with a single click. An example is printing. Instead of having to click 'File', 'Print', then 'OK', we can simply click on the 'Print' icon.

> Macros can save time when you need to repeat the same function over and over again.

These macros have been preset as they are commonly used. If you want other macros, you have to record them yourself. This can be very simple.

To record a macro you need to decide what the macro will do. This needs planning first as every change you make while the macro is recording will be repeated. The macro will work more quickly if you get the steps right first time.

Begley/Sadler Stock Database

Stock Number	4525436
Product name	The Large Present
Manufacturer	The Big Present Company
Sell by date	25/12/2003
Buying price	£29.99
Selling price	£59.99
Supplier	Big Present Suppliers Ltd
Order Contact Number	0555 555555
Packaging	Large brown box
Department	Gifts

Go to Next Record

Once a process has been established, you are ready to record it. To do this in Microsoft Word, select 'Macros' from the 'Tools' menu and click on 'Record new macro'. Make the changes that will be repeated by following the process you have planned, then stop the recording. You need to save and name the macro and then you can make a button to run it.

In some applications, the macro can be used as part of an input process, e.g in a database once a user has input their details, a macro can be used to re-sort the data.

This example of a macro opposite will sort a list into order, save and print the work with the touch of one button. We have planned our macro, so that we know exactly what it will do.

Always give the macro a name that reminds you of what it does, e.g. 'Rank order'.

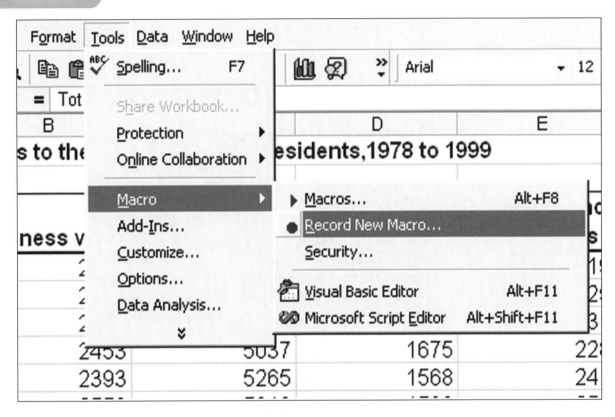

First the macro needs a name, then you can record it. In this case we highlight the data to be sorted, click on 'Data-sort' and select 'Ascending'.

Then we click on the 'Save' button and then finally print. The macro is now recorded. To run the macro, you need to click on 'Tools', then 'Macros'.

Key Points

- Practise the process before you record it to make sure it works.

- Remember, macros are supposed to make the document more user-friendly, not more complex.

- Check that the macro does not already exist in the toolbar.

4.5 Benefits and drawbacks of automation

There are many benefits to using automated processes, which explains why they are used as much as they are. Automating tasks can save time and labour. In the world of business, this is incredibly important as it can save thousands of pounds in the long run. A step repeated many times is always performed quicker when there is only one click needed. Some longer processes can be left to run without an operator. Another advantage is the computer does not get tired or need breaks. If a macro is set up correctly with the correct information, it will not make mistakes.

A bar code reader not only reads the information but it performs calculations and updates the stock control computer. This happens without any further input from the operator.

There are some drawbacks to automating processes. Sometimes, there is a need for manual control when performing delicate processes that require

When automation works, it is superb, but it can be frustrating getting it to this stage.

some response from humans. Macros can be hard to set up and normally take specialist staff and some planning. This takes time, which, of course, costs money. Human input error can cause the same mistake to be repeated many times before it is spotted. If a database is not kept up-to-date, embarrassing mistakes can be made, wasting time, ink and paper.

It's always good to be aware of where computers are used. They are used extensively in manufacturing. A good example is the food industry where many hundreds of the same item are produced on a production line. Not all processes produce a paper end product. Some perform tasks, controlling a mixer or an oven. You might have seen a demonstration of this in a technology lesson.

In the food industry where mass production of a product needs to be as efficient as possible, tasks are performed by machines. It is possible to control a series of these machines using an automated process. The aim of this is to save time starting and stopping the production line, therefore making the process more accurate and efficient.

Key Points

Automated processes save time and labour.

Automated processes take a specialist to set up and need to be planned.

They need to be tested thoroughly before they are used. Mistakes must be corrected at an early stage otherwise disastrous results can occur.

Skills Check

- Can you modify an existing template?
- Can you create and save a document to be used as a template?
- Can you understand the symbols used in a flowchart?
- Can you create a macro?

Progress Check

1 What must you do before starting to record a macro?
2 Why has the development of automated processes meant that there are now some jobs that can be done that couldn't before?
3 Are all automated processes efficient?

1. Write down the order of what you want to record. 2. Some tasks are too dangerous for humans to do and some would take too long. 3. No, sometimes a job is done infrequently and it is not worth setting up the process. Another example is that errors could be corrected automatically that might not need correcting, spellcheck is not always right.

Practice questions

1   State how a computer can be used to speed up routine tasks.

....

....

....

....   **[2 marks]**

2   Planning a project before you start means that you can see all the tasks
    that you need to do.
    How might this affect the order in which you do the tasks?

....

....

....

....   **[2 marks]**

3   What is the purpose of a macro?

....

....

....   **[1 mark]**

Multiple choice questions

1 A flowchart should be used when creating a process because:

    a Teachers always make you use one.
    b It summarises what you have done clearly.
    c It helps you plan what you will do.
    d It proves you can use autoshapes.

2 An automated process would **not** be useful when:

    a Monitoring the temperature of a nuclear reactor core.
    b Typing a letter of resignation to your boss.
    c Opening automatic doors in the entrance to a shop.
    d You need to save your work regularly.

3 Which of the following is **not** an essential feature of a template:

    a Keeping a standard style.
    b Saving time.
    c Easy to use.
    d Lots of colour.

4 What is a macro?

    a A screensaver that starts automatically.
    b An automated process.
    c An automatic reflex action.
    d A small command.

5 Models and modelling

After studying this topic you should be able to:

- use and create automated processes
- draw flowcharts
- represent systems as diagrams
- use and create mail merge
- understand when it is appropriate to automate processes.

5.1 Using automated processes

Whenever you use a computer, you will be using automated processes. These are things that happen when you give a command. The process is pre-programmed, it just needs you to get it started.

An example of an automated process not on a computer is boiling a kettle. You fill it with water and turn it on. This activates the filament which heats up the water, and turns itself off when the thermostat recognises that the water has reached a certain temperature.

> Any time a series of instructions is carried out by the computer after one command from you, the process is automated.

An example of an automated process on a computer is clicking on the print button. After you have pressed print, the computer sends a message to the printer, which automatically grabs the paper and prints the page. See the flowchart on the next page which itemises this process.

These processes are useful as they can save a great deal of time and cut down on humans having to repeat tedious tasks, which can lead to errors as they grow tired and bored. They also save you having to remember complex processes.

Key Points

Automated processes save time.

Humans can have breaks when they need to and leave the computer running.

Don't start an automated process until you have checked that it will work – it will either always be right, or always be wrong.

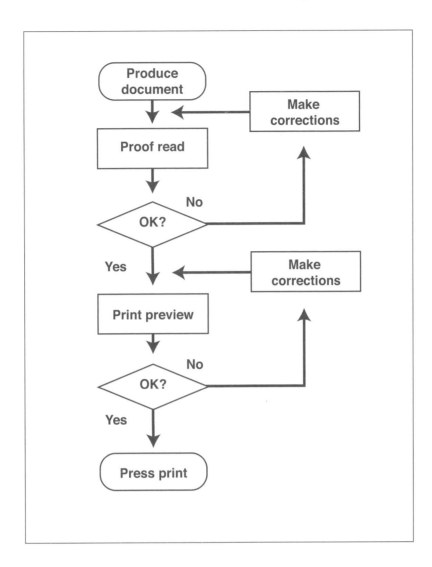

5.2 Creating a process from a series of commands

A very useful skill to help you with any job is to break tasks down into a number of small steps. Each step is called a command, and a procedure is a series of commands. In the early stages of designing a system, it is broken down into commands.

A commonly used example is making a cup of tea. The steps can be written separately:

Fill kettle.

Switch on.

Collect cup, tea, milk, etc.

Add milk to cup.

Add teabag to teapot.

Add boiling water to teapot.

Stir.

Add tea to milk in cup.

Add sugar if required.

Drink carefully as it might be hot.

Once you have written the steps, you need to decide if they are in the proper order. You follow the process through and see if there are any possible bugs in the system. A bug is an overlooked problem, a way in which the system could go wrong – for instance, adding more water to an already full kettle. The skill is then to write the steps in such a way that there can be no doubt as to what happens with each step. The best way to do this is to draw a flowchart. This is covered in the next section.

It is important that other people can follow your process, so it needs to be detailed enough to make sense, but not too detailed so that it is confusing.

> There are lots of things that are more manageable when broken down into smaller chunks – revision is a good example.

Key Points

- Break tasks down into smaller steps.

- The smaller the steps, the less chance of an error.

- If there is a decision to be made, all possibilities must be thought of.

- A series of commands makes a procedure.

5.3 Drawing simple flowcharts

To avoid confusion when reading system diagrams, programmers use a standard system of flowcharts (see topic 4.2). It is usually easier to start a flowchart by writing it out by hand. This is quick and gives you an idea of how to lay it out. The first step is to draw the easiest route through the process in which everything works first time. Add to this any decisions that can be made and check that all possible outcomes have been accounted for.

Planning it on paper saves time later.

Plan your flowchart carefully – it can be hard to alter it later.

When you come to draw the flowchart, you either use specific software or, if you do not have any, 'AutoShapes' in the drawing toolbar of Microsoft Word has a flowchart menu. You can use the shapes and arrows from the toolbar and add text to the boxes by right-clicking on them.

Key Points

Plan your flowchart first.

Check that you have considered all possible outcomes.

Use the correct symbols.

Check that arrows go in the right direction.

5.4 System diagrams

System diagrams generally do not show processes in detail. They give more information about inputs and outputs than a program flowchart does. If you are not sure of the symbols, refer back to Chapter 4.

An example of a system diagram is shown below, demonstrating how a mail merge operation might work.

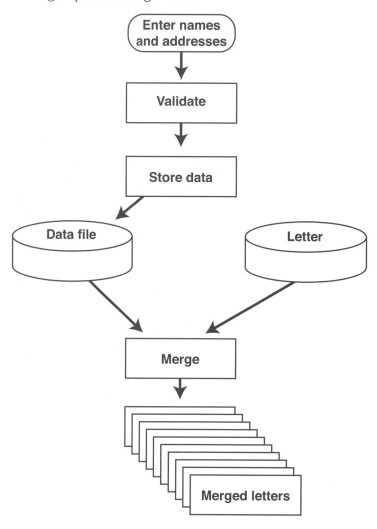

Make sure you keep the labels very brief.

Sometimes it is more appropriate to draw a simple diagram to show how data flows through both the people and computers in a system. This generally gives no detail on how data is stored. See the next page for an example of a data flowchart which shows the process of preparing school reports.

Key Points

Flowcharts can also be useful for non-ICT systems.

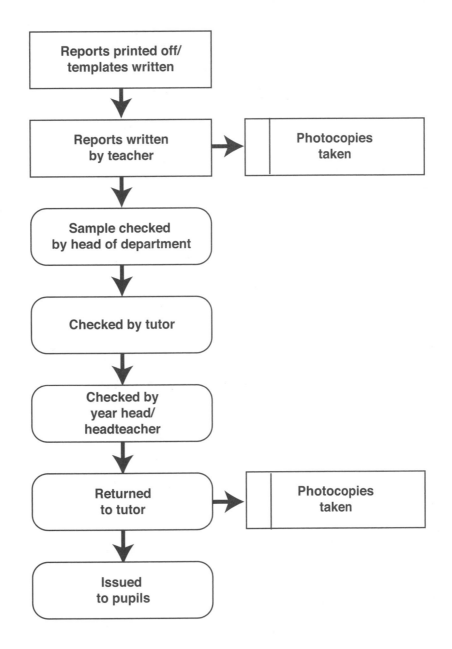

5.5 Mail merge

Have you ever wondered how you or your family seem to get lots of junk mail addressed to you in person? This has only really started to happen in the last 15 years as computer word processors and databases have become more powerful. The tool used to link a database containing personal details to a word processor containing a letter is called mail merge.

The simplest way to set up a mail merge is to write a list of names in a spreadsheet. The next step is to write the letter in a word processor, leaving out the words that are going to be inserted by the mail merge.

> Never be afraid to mail merge, it can save lots of time.

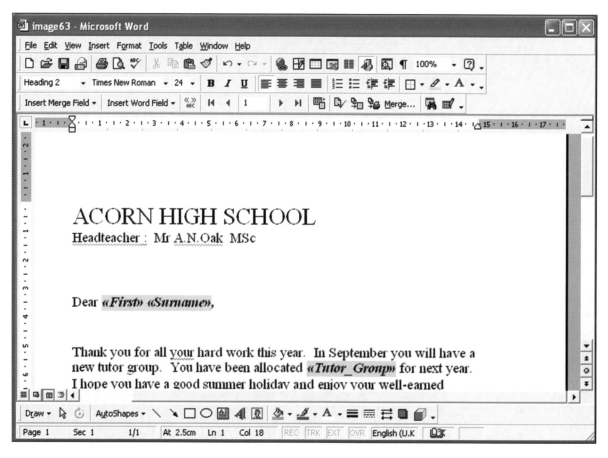

Using 'Mail Merge' in the tools menu you can establish a link between the spreadsheet and the letter. You can then insert 'merge fields', which are the columns in the spreadsheet that will replace the missing words. The computer automatically creates a duplicate letter, inserting the information for each name on the list in the correct place. If you merge words into the wrong place, it is simple to edit the template and re-do the mail merge.

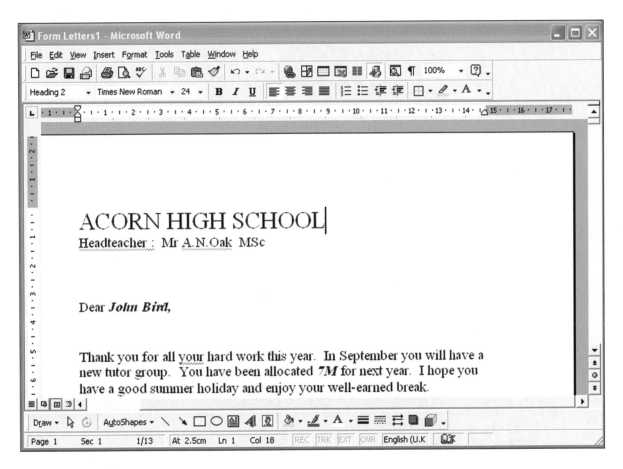

Mail merge is used by companies writing the same letter to lots of clients to give a personal touch to an otherwise general letter. In fact, there are lots of uses, from writing reports, to creating invitations and invoicing customers.

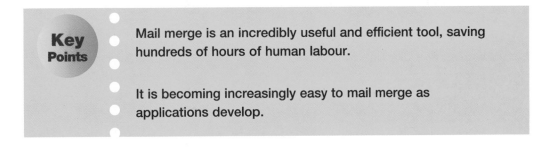

Key Points

Mail merge is an incredibly useful and efficient tool, saving hundreds of hours of human labour.

It is becoming increasingly easy to mail merge as applications develop.

5.6 When to automate processes

It is possible to automate almost any process, but it is not always appropriate to do so. Macros take up memory, can be unnecessarily complicated and can cause applications to crash. In each case, you must decide how useful a macro would really be and whether it will make the task easier. Before deciding to automate the process, think of the advantages and decide whether they outweigh the extra memory used, the slowing down of the machine and the increased potential of the application freezing.

Normally, it is worth automating a process when there is a small job that needs repeating many times. The most obvious example is inserting names from a list on to a letter or invitation. If you didn't mail merge the information, you would either need to copy and paste each name individually, or type them again in the correct place on the page. This is open to human error and is very time-consuming, so it is obviously better to automate the process.

An example of the decision process for another automated process is as follows. You are considering setting up macros at the top of each column on a spreadsheet that, when clicked, sort the data into ascending order for that column.

	A	B	C	D	E	F	G
1				SORT BY No OF BOYS	SORT BY No OFGIRLS	SORT BY TOTAL	Average CAT Score
2							
3	Surname	First	Tutor Group	No of boys	No of girls	Total	Average CAT Score
4	Davidson	Ken	10D	17	14	31	98
5	Southwood	Justin	9X	16	14	30	112
6	Bates	Julie	7X	15	13	28	99
7	Brown	Dave	8A	15	15	30	101
8	Bird	John	7M	14	12	26	100
9	Ireland	Robin	8M	14	14	28	120
10	Platt	Peter	7A	13	17	30	118
11	Walsh	Mike	8X	13	13	26	95
12	Cook	Denis	10E	13	19	32	111
13	Aston	Phil	9M	12	17	29	107
14	Williams	Stuart	10A	12	15	27	116
15	Wall	Justine	9A	11	18	29	89

This macro is a very memory-intensive file and there are lots of things that could potentially go wrong. What have we gained by having these buttons? It might be a simple and very user-friendly way to sort the information, but this task can be completed using three clicks anyway. For a proficient user of spreadsheets, it has no real benefit. For a non-specialist, it could enable them to do a task efficiently with no complex instructions to follow. When considering the user, the decision becomes clear. This is the case with many automated systems.

Always consider who will be using the system.

Skills Check

● Can you draw a diagram to represent a whole system?
● Can you create a mail merge?
● Can you list three reasons why processes can be improved by automation?

Progress Check

1 Why would using a mail merge to send out a club's newsletters save time?
2 Name five things a system should have.
3 Why shouldn't you use too many macros in a file?

1. You could insert the relevant information in the correct place in each letter without typing each one individually. 2. Start, end, input, process and output. 3. The file would become so large that it would be slow to run.

Practice questions

1 Explain why the following system will not work as desired.

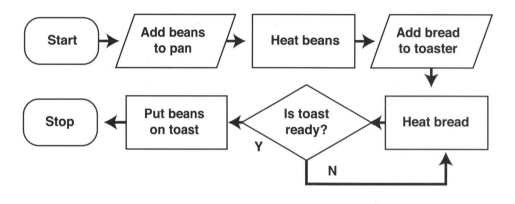

....

.... **[2 marks]**

2 Write down the plan you would produce to show the steps you would take to create a macro to sort a specific column of data alphabetically for future users.

....

....

....

....

.... **[3 marks]**

3 Junk mail is thought to be more successful nowadays as it appears to be more personal. It includes names and addresses and can be made relevant to the receiver.

   a How do companies produce this email?

.... **[1 mark]**

   b Describe how it works.

....

....

.... **[3 marks]**

Multiple choice questions

1 What is a procedure?

    a A series of commands.
    b An essential task.
    c The way a program opens.
    d A loop in a flowchart.

2 In which situation would an automated process benefit you most?

    a Spellchecking.
    b Creating a template.
    c Editing a layout.
    d Making a PowerPoint presentation.

3 What symbols are used to indicate a merged field on a document?

    a < and >
    b " and "
    c « and »
    d ^ and ^

4 Which of the following programs can be used to create a list for mail merging?

    a Word processor.
    b Spreadsheet.
    c Database.
    d All of the above.

5 Which one of the following statements is true?

    a Macros are always an efficient use of time.
    b Macros make work easier for the operator.
    c Macros are useful for routine tasks.
    d A macro takes up less memory than a document would without one.

6 Mail merge is a tool that can be used for:

    a Sending lots of emails simultaneously.
    b Combining two databases.
    c Sorting envelopes for the postman to deliver.
    d Sending personalised marketing mail.

After studying this topic you should be able to:

- use commands
- create a procedure
- use and understand sensors
- test and refine a system
- develop a system
- choose the number of samples
- evaluate the performance of a system
- know about control in society.

6.1 Using commands to create a procedure

Chapter 5 explained how procedures can make life easier and tasks quicker. One example of where this would be useful is computer-aided manufacture (CAM), where machines are given a series of instructions to carry out once they have been activated. This can be seen in very simple control programs, such as Logo and Screen Turtle. A pointer is given instructions to move it around the screen as if viewed from above. It can move with or without drawing lines.

> The simpler the commands, the easier it will be to make it into a procedure later.

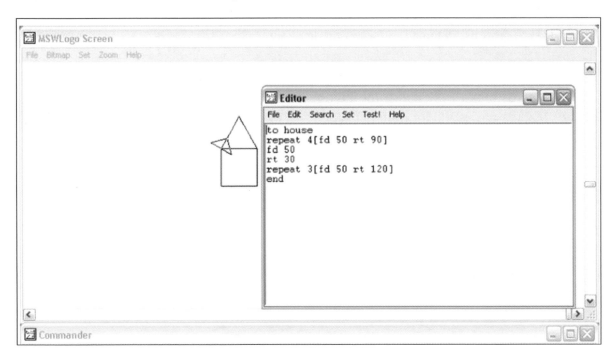

```
to house
repeat 4[fd 50 rt 90]
fd 50
rt 30
repeat 3[fd 50 rt 120]
end
```

A procedure can be made that will combine a series of commands to draw a shape. Using the commands *forward*, *backward*, *left*, *right*, *pen up* and *pen down*, a simple house shape can be drawn.

The image on the previous page was drawn on MSWLogo, a free resource available for download from the Internet.

Key Points

- Have a plan of what you want to do before you start.

- The simpler the procedure, the faster it will run.

- The simpler the procedure, the less memory it will take up.

6.2 Using sensors to measure data

The development of sensors has been one of the really big benefits of using ICT in society. It has saved thousands of hours of mundane work and has made some tasks possible that were impossible previously. One example of a use of sensors is in the monitoring of temperature in all kinds of industries, as many products need to be kept at a constant temperature during production. A more obvious use is in sensors (called thermostats) in cookers and freezers. If the temperature becomes too hot or too cold, a heater or fan can be turned on or off automatically. The Eden Project in Cornwall needs to have a constant environment – humidity must be maintained at all times, otherwise the plants would die. Sensors measure the humidity and the sytem is programmed to add more water as needed.

How did they measure wind speed over a period of time at the North Pole before sensors existed?

A sensor normally consists of the actual measuring device (often called a probe) and the interface, which either stores or converts data.

The apparatus in the photo above can replace the tedious job of measuring the temperature every five minutes with a thermometer. There are many benefits of using sensors for this experiment:

- Releases the operator for other tasks (or a cup of tea!)
- Reduces the risk of human error.
- Increases the accuracy of the measurements and the time they were taken.
- Experiment is less dangerous as chemicals and apparatus are handled less frequently.
- Experiment can take place overnight or for a number of weeks without being constantly monitored by the operator.

Key Points

Sensors are used to save time.

Sensors give more accurate results than humans.

Sensors don't need to take breaks.

Sensors don't become bored.

6.3 Testing and refining a system

Inevitably new systems will have bugs. Do not get a bug confused with a virus. A virus is a program that is specifically written to attach itself to a certain program in the computer and alter the way it runs. A bug is a programming error that causes the program to crash or freeze. An example of a bug is shown in the following flowchart.

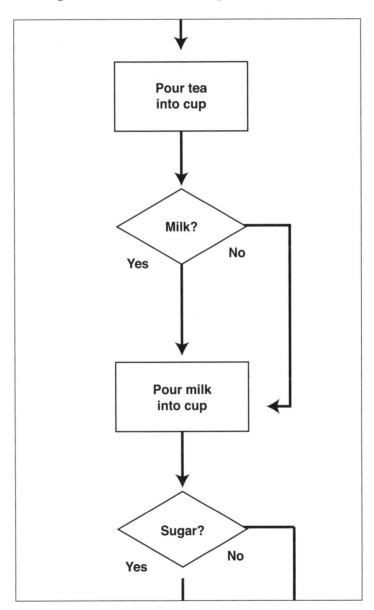

In the example above, you are given milk in your tea whether you like it or not. The point of testing a system is to try to remove all such problems from the system. You need to try every possible outcome and check that the result is as expected.

If there is a bug in the system, part of it will not work and you will need to refine the system. This often means going back to the original plan, looking

The simpler your initial flowchart, the easier it will be to spot bugs, and the easier it will be to adapt the program to remove them.

at the points at which the system failed and trying to work out what needs to be done to solve the problem.

A simple example of a bug is if you are designing a website and there is no way out of a particular page – the user has to either click on 'Back' or close the browser. This can be thought of as a bug. It can be removed by adding a hyperlink back to a home page or another page with links on it.

Key Points

- Whenever a decision is made, you need to test each outcome.

- All routes within the system should have a beginning and an end.

- Once you have refined a system and removed the errors, you should test it again.

6.4 Creating your own system

The most important thing when creating a system is what you do before you start using a computer. You need to write down what you are trying to do and what outcomes you want to achieve. This might involve the collection of information from potential users of your system or from questionnaires sent to users of similar systems.

Once you have planned this, you can start thinking about the flowchart. As mentioned in Chapter 4, a flowchart needs to be as detailed yet as simple as possible. If you follow all the routes carefully and check that every route has a start and an end, you will reduce the number of bugs that might appear.

After you have designed the flowchart you need to think about what the input and output screens will look like. These are the screens that the user will see and into which they will put their data or from which they will print out their results.

> Think about who is going to use your system – who is the audience, what will they want?

It is always good practice to produce two or three designs for each and a final draft explaining why you chose it.

Now that all the planning is done, it is time to implement the system. Consider the software you could use and decide which you will choose, again explaining why. Once you have created the system, you need to create a test plan so that you know it has been thoroughly tested.

Key Points

- Time spent planning will save time later.

- Time spent testing will save time later.

- Consider the skill level of the user when creating the system.

6.5 Evaluating a system

It is a useful skill to be able to evaluate a product. Does it meet your needs? Is there a better product available that will produce similar or better results more efficiently?

When you are looking at a system to solve a problem you must think of some basic targets that the system needs to achieve. If the system meets these targets and it is successful then it can be used; if it fails then bugs may need to be ironed out or a new system may be required. A good system will meet the targets easily and also have plenty of room for the demands of the tasks to grow.

Always be aware of the needs of the system and do not be swayed by unnecessary gimmicks.

A good example of this is online ticket sales. Selling tickets to a small number of people may work well, but when a very popular event takes place the demand may be so high that the system cannot cope with the number of jobs that it has to undertake.

Conversely, if you spend a lot of money on a really powerful system when it only has to handle a small number of tickets, then it is a waste of money.

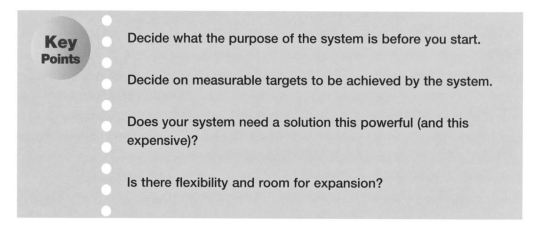

Key Points

- Decide what the purpose of the system is before you start.

- Decide on measurable targets to be achieved by the system.

- Does your system need a solution this powerful (and this expensive)?

- Is there flexibility and room for expansion?

6.6 Control systems in society

There are many types of control systems used every day that we take for granted. Heating comes on automatically at the time we want it or when the temperature falls below a certain level. Traffic lights help ease traffic flow and can respond to demands, and alarms sound to alert us of problems. Try to think of all the control systems you might come across in your average day. Ask yourself why there is a control system, how it was done in the past and why it is better now.

Taking traffic control as an example, at a relatively quiet junction, no control system is necessary. As the number of cars increases, there can be times when a police officer is needed to control the flow of traffic using hand signals. This is how all major junctions were controlled at peak times in the mid-20th century. Now traffic lights have taken this role, a police officer is no longer needed.

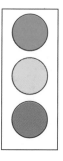

Another good example of a use of a control system is a lighthouse. This is a really important function and any errors can cause disaster, especially as bigger ships are travelling more often. Control systems have affected lighthouses in two ways. Firstly, lighthouses can now be computer controlled, so there is no need for them to be operated by a lighthouse keeper every night – a very lonely job. Secondly, ships' navigation systems have improved with the development of global positioning systems and sensors to detect when they are too near to something (modern cars are beginning to use this technology to help with reversing).

New uses are being thought up all the time for computer control, and this area of ICT is very fast-moving and continually evolving. It can be used for hundreds of tasks, from controlling your cooker to guiding missiles to a target accurately.

It is very unlikely that in Britain today you will spend even one day without interacting with a computer controlled device either knowingly or unknowingly.

Skills Check

- Can you create a series of commands to control something?
- Do you understand what a procedure is?
- Are you aware of how many measurements to take to get reliable results?

Progress Check

1 What is a sensor?
2 Name six different kinds of sensors.
3 Why do some systems have decisions and loops in them?

1. A sensor is a device that measures something. It is connected to a computer via an interface.
2. Temperature, light, sound, pressure, pH, moisture (these are the common ones). 3. To take into account every eventuality.

Practice questions

1 Give examples of how using sensors could improve the manufacture of bread.

....

....

....

....

.... **[3 marks]**

2 Write down the set of commands you would use to produce the outline of a French flag using Logo.

....

....

....

....

....

.... **[3 marks]**

3 State five benefits/drawbacks of using sensors.

....

....

....

....

.... **[5 marks]**

Multiple choice questions

1 Which of the following **cannot** be measured by a sensor?

    a Pressure.
    b Motion.
    c Weight.
    d Reliability.

2 Which of the following commands would **not** work in a Logo program?

    a forward
    b fd
    c Pen up
    d Up

3 Which would be the best type of sensor to use in a freezer?

    a Temperature sensor.
    b Pressure sensor.
    c Smoke sensor.
    d Noise sensor.

4 Which of the following is **not** a use of control in everyday life?

    a Speed camera.
    b Barcode reader.
    c Automatic doors.
    d Cats eyes on the road.

5 Which of the following is **not** a benefit directly related to control systems?

    a More efficient offices.
    b More accurate measurements.
    c Saving operator hours on routine jobs.
    d Non-stop measurements, as computers don't need breaks.

After studying this topic you should be able to:

- recognise common forms used in communications
- address the needs of an audience
- apply the correct conventions to your work
- recognise the effectiveness of your work against given criteria
- understand the differing impact of different presentation techniques
- devise criteria to appraise a presentation.

7.1 Using the correct style

22 Acacia Avenue
Claw Street
Bristol
BS40 3RU

28/09/2003

Internet Perfection Ltd
4 The Strand
Wilmslow
Herts
WM3 4RS

Dear sirs

Re: account no. 37467895

I wish to terminate my contract for internet access with you forthwith. Please ensure that no further payments are taken from my account and confirm by return of letter that this request has been actioned.

Yours faithfully

Richard Wursley

---

22 Acacia Avenue,
Claw Stoke
Bristol BS40
23/07/03

Dear Max

Thank you very much for the wedding present. The large inflatable swimming pool will come in really useful in the long hot summer we are expecting. Hope you enjoyed the day.

Yours sincerely,
David + Rachel.

It is important when making a document to be aware of the style. How should your document be laid out? There are standard ways of laying out certain types of document. An example of this is a letter. When typing a letter, everything should be aligned to the left. This reduces time rearranging things on a page if many letters have to be typed. Your address appears at the top or top right of the page, and the address of the person being written to should always appear at the top left, followed by the date, a salutation (*Dear Susan*) and finally the content of the letter. This layout is different from when you write a letter by hand, as it's easier to move your pen around the page rather than the cursor.

Some documents will have a similar style, whether produced on a computer or by hand. A good example of this is a poster, which should always have large eye-catching fonts and images and use bright colours. There is a standard format to a report, whether at school or in business. This is title, author and date, executive summary (a paragraph briefly describing the whole report), then the introduction. The introduction sets the scene for the rest of the report, and is followed by the main topics discussed and at the end an evaluation or conclusion.

> Try to use this format in all the reports that you write.

Newspapers have their own style – whether they are tabloids or broadsheets, the front page will have a certain format:

- Name of the newspaper at the top
- Price and date
- Headline
- A large photo
- A leader (an article continued inside which draws you into the newspaper), with text in columns
- Contents at the bottom
- A bar code (Unique Product Code – UPC)

Inside a newspaper, there will still be photos, but they are less likely to be in colour. There will be more text in separate sections divided into columns. There will probably be adverts on most pages and each page will be clearly numbered. Usually, sections will be divided by lines.

When producing a document it is important to consider what the accepted style is. If you do not keep to the style, your reader might be confused and find the document difficult to read. This will defeat the object of your document, as people could stop reading before the end and miss the point.

Key Points

- Think about the style before starting.
- A rough sketch of the layout will save time later.
- Look at similar documents before you start yours.
- Try to be consistent throughout the document and with others, if you produce more than one.

7.2 Giving the right impression

Once you have chosen a suitable layout, you need to think about what type of content you will include. Ask yourself who you are aiming the document at. Who will the audience be? What impression do you want to give? For example, if you were producing an article about terrorism and its effect on the world today, the audience would not expect to see cartoon images. Photos would probably be used in addition to the text about this serious topic. If you had cartoons, people might think the document was trivial and not read it. Alternatively, if you were writing a light-hearted story, but the layout was not eye-catching and the pictures too formal, people might be put off, as they would expect it to be entertaining.

Always be aware of the visual impression your document gives. Does it match the type of document?

Can you see how the two images opposite would affect how an article would be perceived by the reader?

Key Points

Think about what you are trying to say.

Think about how you want the audience to react when they see the document.

Remember, first impressions are really important.

7.3 Does your work do the job?

Before you finish a task you should decide if it meets the requirements that have been set out at the start. To do this you need to review and evaluate your work. Imagine, for example, that you are producing a website for a company. The company would specify details at the beginning of the project for you to include. These might be using the company colour scheme, including the company logo and aiming the website at teenagers. Before showing the website to the company, you would need to evaluate the website, making sure you have met all these specifications. If you found that the website missed out one or two key requirements then you could improve the website before showing it to the company.

Evaluating your work is vital at GCSE level.

This is the same procedure that you should follow when producing any work to be handed in.

Evaluation fits into the design process as shown in the diagram below.

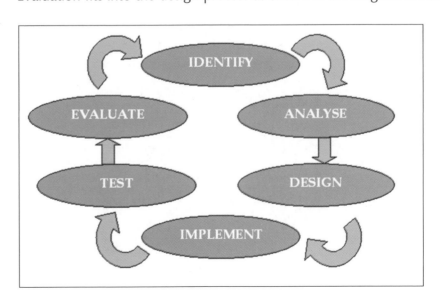

If you know that your work meets all the requirements set out, then it is likely that the reader will be impressed – and if it is school work, you are more likely to get a high mark. This is not exclusively an ICT skill, it is transferable to every subject and also to everyday life.

Key Points

- Before finishing a task, look back to the original question, brief or specification.

- Tick off the requirements as you identify them.

- If there is something missing, go back and check whether you have actually done it, but not shown the evidence. If you have missed it out, then add it.

7.4 Different ways of presenting information

Traditionally, the main method of presenting information was to write it on paper, by hand or using a typewriter. Over the last few years, many other ways of presenting information have become popular. This has happened because of wider accessibility of computers and the development of presentation packages. The price of the hardware needed has dramatically reduced, making televisions, videos, video recorders and data projectors more affordable.

Keep an eye on the price of a piece of hardware for six months – see how it changes before the item is replaced by the next model.

Don't feel that you are restricted to writing an essay to present information (unless this is specified). Sometimes it would be more appropriate to make a video, produce a website or create a PowerPoint presentation. The question is what medium to choose – what is most appropriate for the subject matter and audience (not what would be most fun to produce)? Ask yourself these five questions:

1 What is the purpose?
2 Who is the audience?
3 How could it be delivered?
4 What resources do I have?
5 How long do I have to do it?

The coach shown in the picture above probably spent a lot time making the presentation, but it was not necessary. He could have got the point across just as well by talking and using a chalkboard. He could also have handed out a page of notes for each child to read – but this would have been even less appropriate.

If you had to produce a weather forecast for a school trip, you might choose to use a PowerPoint presentation and make a video recording with a presenter explaining the slides. This would look much more professional than an essay or an Excel spreadsheet, which could give all the information needed. But is it really necessary or helpful?

- List all the ways you could present the information to the required audience.

- Decide which ones you can realistically do in the time given.

- Consider which of these would be most effective.

- Choose the best presentation method, which might not necessarily be the easiest or most fun to produce.

7.5 Making your own targets

Some tasks are very general and do not give specific targets. A target is a question about your work that can only be answered by testing it. If you are not given targets this does not mean that there shouldn't be any. You should decide what the important factors are and make up your own targets. Obvious targets that will apply to most pieces of work are:

- Is it all spelled correctly?

- Have I answered the question or done what was specified?

- Can it be read easily?

- Have I met the needs of the audience?

- Does it look finished?

- How much blank space is there?

Make your targets SMART: Specific, Measurable, Achievable, Realistic and Timed.

If you set too many targets it can be unrealistic and make your work seem designed to meet the targets rather than flowing naturally.

Every target you set yourself must have a clear way of being measured. For instance, the question 'Is the language appropriate for a Year 7 student?' can be measured by getting a Year 7 student to read it and underline the words they don't understand. Alternatively, you could use the readability score and check that the reading age is appropriate. The most reliable method would be to get a sample of Year 7 students from across the ability range to read your work.

Once you have written your targets, do not adapt them so that they match up with your work, stick to the original targets.

Key Points

- Make your targets realistic.

- Make your targets measurable.

- Do not change the targets unless the specifications change.

Skills Check

- Do you know how to set up standard documents?
- Can you explain why certain applications are better for certain specific tasks?
- Are you aware of the different ways that you can present information?
- Do you understand what is meant by a critical evaluation of a presentation?

Progress Check

1 Describe what you would expect to see on the front page of a newspaper.
2 What two things must you think of before starting any document?
3 How else can you present information other than by writing an essay?

1. Title, price, date, headline, sub heading, main article, (and possibly) second article, contents, leader.
2. The layout and the audience. 3. PowerPoint presentation, website, talk, video, magazine article, poster, leaflet, etc.

Practice questions

1 a What typifies a good word-processed, professional business letter?

....

....

....　**[3 marks]**

b How will it differ from a hand-written letter and why?

....

....

....

....

....　**[3 marks]**

2 Which of the following would be an important factor when making a document for the following audiences? Link the factor to the audience.

Young child   Catchy title
Sports club member   Bright colours
Professional   Technical jargon
Technician ———   Relevant pictures
Teenager   More text than image　**[4 marks]**

3 Why is it important to have measurable targets? Give two examples of these.

....

....

....

....

....　**[3 marks]**

Multiple choice questions

1 A standard layout for a letter does **not** need to contain:

   a Sender's address.
   b Subject.
   c Date.
   d Signature.

2 A magazine page template should **always** include:

   a Picture.
   b Headline.
   c Date.
   d Space for a picture.

3 A good target for a piece of work would be:

   a Finish it by the deadline.
   b Be nice about everything in the work.
   c Try your hardest.
   d Make it fair when you are working in a pair.

4 A SMART target stands for:

   a Small and right.
   b Specific, measurable, achievable, realistic and timed.
   c Specific, medium, average, regular target.
   d Spontaneous, measurable, agreeable, realistic target.

5 Which of the following is **not** a good way of giving information to a large audience?

   a A video.
   b A PowerPoint presentation.
   c A Word document.
   d A speech using a microphone.

8 Refining and presenting information

After studying this topic you should be able to:

- plan and design a presentation
- capture images to improve a presentation
- structure your work effectively
- import and export information
- understand the limitations of the computer you are using
- choose the correct software.

8.1 Planning and designing a slide presentation

Think before you begin.

When planning a presentation it is always a good idea to note down a rough plan to start with. First of all decide what message you are trying to put over. Are you trying to inform people of something, advertise an event or sell something? The objective of your presentation will change the structure and the way you deliver it.

Once you have considered what you are trying to do, then you need to consider your audience. Your language, fonts, pictures and sound will change depending on who you want to communicate with. Generally, presentations for children will have larger fonts, brighter colours and less text. Presentations for the elderly will also have larger fonts and possibly a less complex design.

 Key Points

Always produce a rough plan before you start.

Think about your audience.

Ask yourself what you are trying to achieve.

8.2 Structuring a slide presentation

After planning the presentation, you need to think how to structure it. It's important to be aware of how long you've got to talk for and how much information you have to get across. Try to work out how many slides you need and compare that with how long you wish to talk. This gives you an average amount of time each slide is shown for. Some slides will obviously need less time than others, but this will give you an idea of whether you are going to fill the time.

> Calculate how many slides per minute you want to show.

For example, if you have to do a five minute presentation and it can be broken down into ten slides, the average will be two slides per minute. Some slides may take more and some less, but if they all need less time, then you need to think about making more slides.

Like any good piece of work, your presentation should be constructed in a logical manner, with a beginning, middle and end. The beginning should give the audience an idea of what you are about to tell them and should try to catch their interest. The middle should contain the main content and any evidence to back up the conclusions being made. The end should summarise what you have said and emphasise the key points. There is no set number of slides in a beginning, middle or end – it will depend on how much information you choose to put on each slide.

You should always take care that each slide does not look cluttered. Don't use too much text, too many images or too many animations.

The images above show two slides from a similar presentation about the same subject. It is easy to see how important information can be lost to the reader if the slide is too cluttered. For example, if you just saw the first slide, would you have noticed that there is free cheese tasting at the Frome Cheese Show?

Once you have planned the content of your presentation, arrange your slides so that there are images or graphs spaced fairly evenly throughout the presentation – to break up long blocks of text and give the audience something different to look at.

If there is no way to avoid having long blocks of text, try to summarise the key issues using bullet points, as these are much easier to read than paragraphs.

Another way to hold the audience's interest is to use a consistent style throughout the presentation with well-planned combinations of colours. It always looks better if all the titles are in the same font, all the paragraphs have the same font and all the backgrounds are the same.

Key Points

- Always have a beginning, a middle and an end.

- Plan carefully what will be on each slide.

- Space out pictures and graphs evenly, if possible.

- Use bullet points to break up long blocks of text.

- Don't spend all your time getting the background colours just right.

8.3 Selecting and capturing images

Use of images is very important in presentations. Images are not just used to illustrate a point or to show what something looks like, they are also used to bring balance to a presentation and to give the audience something to look at to hold their interest. If you are giving a presentation, you often feel better if the audience is not looking at you, and they would be more likely to look away from you to an image than to look at text.

You should consider carefully each image and where it will be placed. In topic 7.2 we looked at what the audience would expect to see. Usually an image would be selected because it is relevant to the presentation. However, sometimes an unexpected image can be used to catch the audience's attention or shock them. This will help them to remember certain details more easily.

> Something surprising often makes a presentation really memorable.

When setting out the page you must think about the size of the images. If an image is too large then this might detract from the impact of the text, but if it's too small then it might lose the impact it is trying to make – either because it looks too insignificant or because it is too small to be seen clearly.

Key Points

- Be aware of the audience when choosing a picture.

- Choose a picture relevant to the presentation.

- Make sure the image is sized appropriately.

8.4 Transferring information

It is often useful to be able to transfer information from one application into another. Generally, this can be done by copying and pasting. Firstly, you need to select the information you require. Use one of the many methods of copying, place the cursor where you want the selection to go and use one of the many methods of pasting.

This works well when the applications can be opened at the same time and the computer is not slowed down too much by running the programs. If you are not sure whether your computer can handle a large image, it's often better to save it first. You can then insert the picture at a later date. You'll have various options to save, as can been seen here:

> You can copy by using the 'Edit' drop-down menu, by holding down 'Control' and pressing 'C' or by right-clicking to get the correct pop-up menu.

```
Open Link
Open Link in New Window
Save Target As...
Print Target

Show Picture
Save Picture As...
E-mail Picture...
Print Picture...
Go to My Pictures
Set as Background
Set as Desktop Item...

Cut
Copy
Copy Shortcut
Paste

Add to Favorites...

Properties
```

Information can be obtained from the Internet in the same way but text does not always copy in a suitable style for your purpose. This is because most websites include tables (normally with invisible borders). This allows the website designer to place things exactly where they want them. The table is often copied with the text. It's simple to convert this to a normal text document by using the 'Table' drop-down menu.

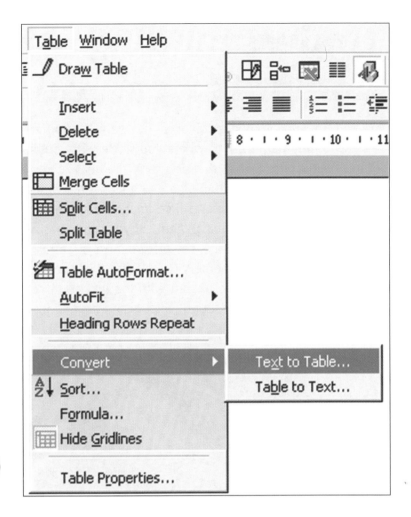

Attaching files and choosing the best types of file is covered in Chapter 9.

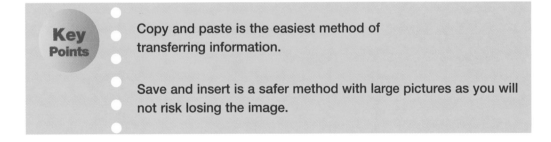

Key Points

Copy and paste is the easiest method of transferring information.

Save and insert is a safer method with large pictures as you will not risk losing the image.

8.5 Understanding what your computer can do

Imagine you have to collect five parcels of different weights and sizes and bring them back to where you started. It would be better to pick up the light ones first so that you carry the heavy ones for less time. In the same way, when constructing a multimedia presentation, do not always start off by placing the pictures first. Images are memory intensive and so can be considered the 'heavy' items. If your page has a big picture on it, whenever you reload the page, the picture must be refreshed. This takes up a lot of random access memory (RAM) and therefore slows down your computer. It would be sensible to start with the text and once you have completed this, add the pictures, sound, colours and animations.

Think about why your computer suddenly starts running slowly – what have you just done?

The parts of the computer to do with speed are the processor and the RAM. The processor sorts the information and decides what to do with it. The RAM deals with how much information can be processed at any one time. Dealing with larger files or pictures takes up more RAM, making your computer run more slowly.

Sometimes it is important to consider how much memory you will need to save the file. If you are planning to transfer the file between computers by floppy disk, the file must remain below 1.4 megabytes in total. There are ways round this by using compression programs, such as Winzip or Zip central, through which files can be compressed and also spanned across a number of disks. An easier way to avoid this problem is to use a writeable CD (if your computer has a CD drive) which can hold 640 megabytes of memory, or a memory stick. If you want to transfer files by email (see Chapter 9) you need to be aware of how to minimise the file size to reduce the transfer time.

Key Points

When producing a document, put the pictures in last.

If your computer is running slowly, give it less to do.

Think about file size if you are going to transfer something from one computer to another.

8.6 Choosing the correct application

After you have identified a task, you need to decide which would be the most effective application to use. The easiest way to do this is to think of what you are trying to produce. You might decide to use a word processing package if you are going to:

Sometimes it is hard to decide whether to use a word processor or DTP software.

- produce a document containing mainly text
- add contents pages and a standard style for headings.

You would probably decide to use a desktop publishing package (DTP) if you want to:

- produce a poster
- produce a document heavily based on a template, such as a magazine page
- produce a banner, CD cover, newsletter or website.

A **spreadsheet** would be used when you need to:

- do lots of calculations
- model something to see what would happen
- produce graphs
- have an easy way of sorting or filtering information.

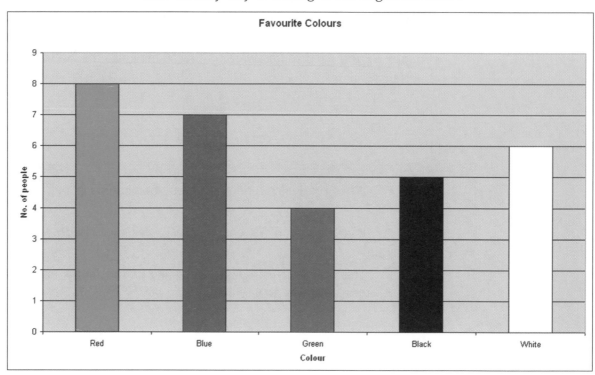

Other applications that need to be considered are **presentation** packages like PowerPoint, **web creation** software such as Frontpage, Dreamweaver or HotMetal Pro or **database** software such as Access, Flexidata or Pinpoint. Each has its own merits. Some have a similar interface to other applications you might be familiar with.

When explaining why you chose a particular software package, you also need to say why you didn't choose other applications, thereby showing good all-round knowledge.

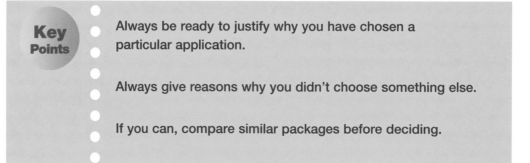

Key Points

- Always be ready to justify why you have chosen a particular application.

- Always give reasons why you didn't choose something else.

- If you can, compare similar packages before deciding.

Skills Check

- Can you design a presentation that is effective for the target audience and the required purpose?
- Do you know all the ways to obtain images?
- Can you draw an appropriate layout for a given task?

Progress Check

1 Name five ways to obtain images for use in a document.
2 How do you choose the right software to use?
3 When would you create a template?

1. Scan, take photo, draw using illustration software, download from the Internet or a CD-ROM, draw with vector graphics, draw on paper and scan it in. 2. Decide which would produce the best output in the most efficient way. 3. When you might want to adapt the document in the future for further use.

Practice questions

1 Give five ways of acquiring images to place in a document.

....

....

.... **[5 marks]**

2 To stop a slide being too cluttered, you need some areas of blank space.
   This is called white space (whatever the colour of the background).
   When making a magazine cover, why is it important where this white
   space is on the page?

....

....

.... **[2 marks]**

3 Choose the application you would use for each of the following documents.
   Link the document to the application you would use.

   Newspaper front page   Spreadsheet
   Letter   Desktop publisher
   Website   Slide show software
   Cash flow forecast   Web creation software
   Presentation   Word processor   **[4 marks]**

4 What factors might limit the ability of a computer to perform a certain task?

....

....

.... **[3 marks]**

Multiple choice questions

1 White space, in page design, is:

    a Always white.

    b Used to break up the page.

    c Used to fill up space.

    d Always a bad thing.

2 It is **not** necessary for a presentation to be:

    a Specific to the audience.

    b Structured.

    c Very loud.

    d Relevant.

3 You never need to worry about copyright when getting an image from:

    a A digital camera.

    b A scanner.

    c The Internet.

    d A CD-ROM.

4 What is ROM in a computer?

    a The working memory.

    b The same as RAM.

    c When files are stored on a computer.

    d A drive on a computer.

5 What might make your computer run very slowly when your document is open?

    a Lack of hard disk space.

    b Low amount of RAM.

    c Font too big.

    d Old version of the application.

⑨ Communicating

After studying this topic you should be able to:

- use email
- know how to be secure on the Internet
- understand the technical issues involved in data transfer
- adapt material for different audiences
- use the correct file types
- use email address books
- create hyperlinks and select favourites
- understand some of the moral and social issues surrounding electronic communication.

9.1 Using email and address books

For thousands of years, people have sent written messages to each other. In Roman times, small wooden tablets with messages on them were taken by slaves from person to person, ordering stock, transferring information and inviting people to dinner. Throughout the ages, the speed of delivery has dramatically increased. This has been achieved by advances in transport. From foot and horse to road and rail and then aeroplane, the time it took to deliver a message has been reduced. But, in essence, the only aspects of the delivery system that had changed were the introduction of postage stamps in the mid-19th century and postcodes in the last century.

As it is easier and cheaper to send messages, be prepared to receive unwanted emails.

However, everything changed with the development of the Internet and email. Nowadays, lots of people have access to email and can send and receive messages almost instantly via the Internet.

Most email systems have a similar format. You will need to know your own email address and the password to access your email account as well as the email address of the person or organisation you are sending the message to. Most screens where you type your message look similar.

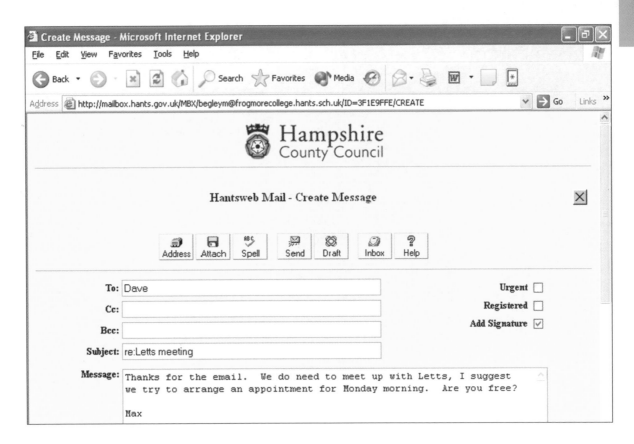

At the top, you need to write the address of the person you are sending the message to. You can copy the message to someone else by using 'cc' (carbon copy) or you can copy it to someone else without the receiver knowing, using 'bcc' (blind carbon copy). The next line is usually 'subject' and this is very important. All emails you send must include a subject, as it is the only thing other than your address that the receiver will see before they open it. This allows the receiver to filter unwanted emails and decide which are most important to open first.

To save time and to avoid having to remember or look up everybody's email address, most accounts will allow you to use an electronic address book, which is part of the email software. This means that you can either select who you will send the message to from the address book, or by writing in a 'quickname' rather than writing the whole address. See the image on the next page for an example of email quickname.

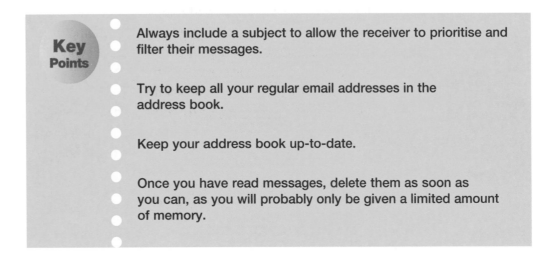

Key Points

Always include a subject to allow the receiver to prioritise and filter their messages.

Try to keep all your regular email addresses in the address book.

Keep your address book up-to-date.

Once you have read messages, delete them as soon as you can, as you will probably only be given a limited amount of memory.

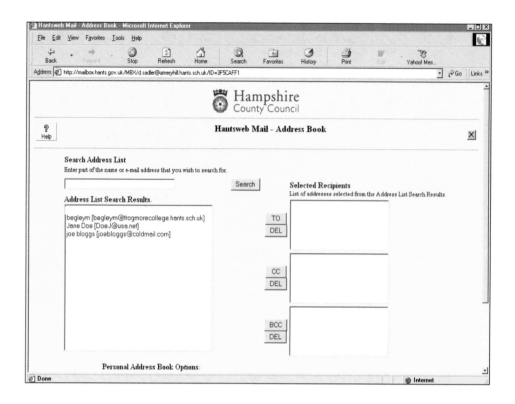

9.2 Keeping yourself safe

Just as many people receive junk mail through the post, it is likely you will receive junk mail, known as spam, at your email address . Most of these emails will probably be harmless advertisements for mortgages or loans.

However, there is a possibility that you might get an email that has a virus attached to it. Therefore it is very important to check the sender before opening any email, and especially before opening any attachments.

There are two main types of virus. First there is a program that is designed to destroy or modify files or applications on your computer. Some of these are very simple and they will just destroy a file, while others can be extremely complex and can duplicate themselves and send viruses to other people using your address book. An example of this is the 'love bug' which came out in 2001. Second, there is a program called a 'Trojan' named after the Trojan horse in Greek mythology. A Trojan is a program that will attach itself to an email and install itself onto your computer, allowing the writer of the program to access your computer and everything on it whenever you are online. Trojans even have the ability to stop you from using the computer. The only way to deal with such a virus is either not to use the Internet in the rirst place, or to reformat the computer to delete the virus.

There are simple methods of avoiding catching a computer virus:

1 Only give your email address to people you trust.

2 Install a virus checker and keep it up-to-date.

3 Delete any emails from people you don't know.

4 Listen out for information about viruses in the press.

5 Don't open attachments from emails that have been forwarded.

6 Block unwanted emails using a filtering system.

Most email accounts have a way of filtering out undesirable emails and spam. Spam is junk mail, and companies rely on a tiny percentage of people opening the email and acting on it. It is a cheap way to advertise their company and to draw attention to their products. Undesirable emails consist of anything from viruses and trojans to pornographic material. There are different ways to filter emails. You can set up your system so that it only allows you to receive emails from people in your address book, which is useful for young children. Alternatively, you can set up your system so that it does not allow you to receive mass emails to a general email address. You can also block messages from individual accounts, but most mailing companies get around this by changing their email address regularly.

Key Points

- Keep an eye out for unfamiliar addresses.

- Be careful about what attachments you open.

- If you have important information on your computer, back it up and keep it somewhere safe.

9.3 How information is transferred using the Internet

The Internet is not just useful for finding information. You can also use it to download programs and other types of file on to your computer. The information can be downloaded from a server that a company controls. People may decide to make files available for download if they think other people might use them and there is no copyright problem. They can create a shared area on their computer and allow access to it via a standard modem, ISDN or broadband (ADSL) connection.

> The faster the connection speed, the more expensive it is.

If you are downloading lots of information or big files, the speed of download is really important. Each document is broken down into very small parts and then transferred using the telephone connection. The speed of transfer is measured by the baud rate, in kilobytes per second or megabytes per second. A typical modem will have a baud rate of 56 kb/s, an ISDN line has 125 kb/s and broadband can vary from 250 kb/s up to 2 Mb/s.

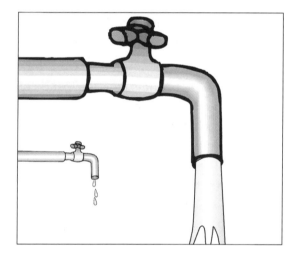

In the diagram, more water can pass through the thicker pipe in the same amount of time. This is a good analogy for Internet connections – more information can pass down a broadband line than a modem line in the same amount of time (even though the cables are actually the same size).

Key Points

Think about the size of what you are sending or downloading. Is using the Internet the most efficient way of doing it bearing in mind your connection speed?

Always weigh up the cost versus time saved. Is it really worth spending the extra money on broadband if you only download one or two programs or other files a month?

9.4 Presenting information for a wider audience

When analysing a task, one of the aspects that you need to look at is the audience it is intended for, as discussed in previous chapters. This is particularly true of technical or specialised documents. If you are producing a leaflet to explain how to look after your mountain bike, you might be very technical, specifying all the technical requirements. This would make it difficult to understand for beginners, who might be put off by the 'techno babble'.

It is important to realise that other people, less informed than yourself, might like to read the document too. This is why modern electronic equipment (e.g. video recorders) usually have a 'quick start' guide as well as the technical guide, so that those who only want to use the basic functions can get started straightaway.

The language used in the quick start guide is simplified for all to understand and is probably laid out in bullet points so that it is easy to follow. It is worth considering a section like this in your work, either an introduction or a summary, to make it more accessible to everybody.

> Bullet points make your work easier to follow when used occasionally to set out a series of points or instructions.

As the old saying goes, one picture is worth a thousand words. Illustrations in your work make the information more accessible to those who cannot read well and make it more interesting to look at for the young. Going one stage further, if your pictures can move, you can include an element of surprise and show even more information. For example, you might be demonstrating a sporting technique which would be difficult to explain in words and take lots of still images to show. The BBC do this well in the sport section of their website. Different ways to present animated information include PowerPoint presentations, websites or videos.

9.5 Attachments and file types

There are many different file types for each kind of information. An image might be a bitmap, jpeg, tif, gif or psd file. Most file types are known by their three-letter file extension code – the letters that appear after the dot at the end of the file name. A bitmap is shortened to bmp, a jpeg to jpg.

Other common file extensions are:

doc text file (Microsoft)

txt plain text file (all applications)

rtf rich text format (all applications)

pub DTP file (Microsoft)

xls spreadsheet file (Microsoft)

csv spreadsheet file/list (all applications)

mdb database file (Microsoft)

ppt presentation file (Microsoft)

It is important to be aware of the different file types because some take up much less memory and are therefore quicker to transfer between computers. Others work on all applications and are therefore more likely to work on other computers as they are more likely to have the correct software.

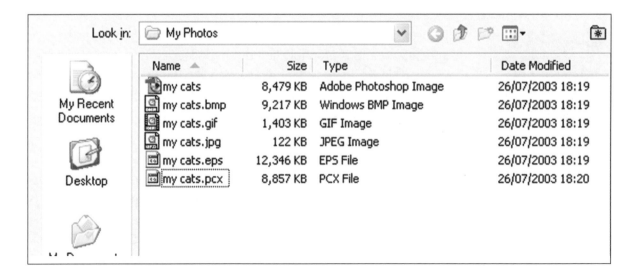

When attaching a file to an email, think about who will download it and whether speed is an issue.

Which file in the folder opposite do you think will download faster from an email? Obviously it will be the smallest file.

Key Points

- Generally, if you are looking for a quality image, keep the file size large.

- Files to be transferred need to be as small as possible without making the quality too low.

- Try to be aware of the specification of the computer receiving the file – older programs will not open newer files, and not everyone uses Microsoft Office.

9.6 Moral and social issues surrounding electronic communication

Nowadays, information is generally stored on computer.
This is better than storing it on paper for a number of reasons.
Information stored on computer:

- takes up less space

- can be updated at any time

- can be accessed from any computer via the Internet

- is more portable

- is easier to search.

So there are obviously lots of benefits. However, with benefits come many disadvantages:

- Information can easily be lost unless it is backed up regularly.

- Files can be corrupted.

- Hackers can steal information.

- Viruses can infect the system.

- Personal information can get into the wrong hands.

- Old information can be stored and treated as if it were up-to-date.

The Data Protection Act was brought in to try to stop the misuse of electronic data in 1984. It was updated in 1998 because of the increased use of the Internet.

Another major social issue is that some people do not have access to computers or the Internet, so if you only give information that way, it might be perceived as unfair. Also, less computer literate people would not be able to communicate as effectively using electronic means. They would receive information much more slowly by post ('snail mail') and might miss out on something.

Other issues are becoming increasingly important, such as the sharing of files. Downloading music files from the Internet or copying them onto CD or minidisc involves breaking copyright laws. It has a negative effect on the music industry if people copy music rather than buying it.

If the files being shared are images, again there are likely to be copyright issues, and other laws concerning child protection and privacy might be broken. This is of particular concern when using chatrooms, as not everyone in the chatroom might be exactly who they say they are.

The world has in a sense become a smaller place and communication has become almost instant. Many companies only advertise online, and the only way to obtain their goods or services is via the Internet. People pay online using credit cards and demand service faster. The pace of life is quicker, making things more stressful and people more tired.

There are advantages to electronic communications in the workplace as, although the pace is faster, it does allow people to work from home, eliminating travelling time (and reducing road congestion) so the working day can be shorter.

> Don't give out personal information in chatrooms. If you get to know someone in a chatroom, never arrange to meet up with them on your own.

Key Points

- Be careful when putting any personal information on the Internet – think about whether it could be misused. For example, don't say you are going on holiday and give your home address, as someone might read it and burgle your house.

- Try to keep up-to-date with the latest communications technology.

- Don't be ignorant of the laws – know what you can and can't download.

- Can you use email, including attachments?
- Can you set up an address book?
- Can you save a file in the best way to transfer it?
- Can you create a hyperlink?
- Are you aware of the potential risks of communicating via the Internet?

Progress Check

1 When sending a file over the Internet, what should you consider?
2 Which file types would be better to use to email a photo to your grandparents?
3 What information should you not give out in a chatroom?

1. The size of the file, the specification of the machine you are sending it to and the knowledge of the user. 2. jpg, gif or tif. 3. Personal information.

Practice questions

1 a Why would it be useful to convert bitmap files to jpeg files?

.... **[1 mark]**

b When would it be useful to use a jpeg file rather than a bitmap?

.... **[1 mark]**

2 What are the dangers of giving out your personal details over the Internet?

....

....

....

....

.... **[3 marks]**

3 Give three ways that the increased use of email has affected the way that businesses run today.

....

....

....

....

.... **[3 marks]**

Multiple choice questions

1 What should you keep private when using an Internet chatroom?

    a Your first name.
    b The colour of your hair.
    c Your address.
    d Your email address.

2 Which file would tend to be the largest?

    a .tif
    b .jpg
    c .pcx
    d .bmp

3 Which file type is best for transferring text from one computer to another, when you don't know what applications the second computer is running?

    a .doc
    b .rtf
    c .pub
    d .xls

4 What sort of program would allow an unwanted user to access your computer?

    a Frozen horse.
    b Caesar.
    c Virus.
    d Trojan.

5 Why must you think before putting a photograph of yourself on the Internet?

    a It takes up a lot of hard disk space.
    b It will be available to undesirable people.
    c It might be too pixelated.
    d Your friends might see it.

10 Coursework case studies

After studying this topic you should be aware of:

- how to present a project
- how to spot the key points
- what the teacher is looking for.

Introduction

The ICT work that you cover throughout Key Stage 3 is project based. This means that you will collect information as you do the work and hand in evidence of how you did the work and why you made the choices that you did as you went along. This is just as important as the finished article for the teacher as it will help them to decide how your ICT skills are progressing.

There are two projects included in this book. They are not designed to show the ideal solution to any work that your teacher has set you, nor are they there so that they can simply be copied. The idea is that you can see the two pieces of work and look at how they have been done.

The first project is a Year 7 task about producing a leaflet. The leaflet itself is not the important thing in this book, the mark scheme is. This explains what the teacher is looking for and how they will be marking it. There are marks for how good it looks, but more important is whether it's doing the job it's supposed to do.

The second project is a Year 9 case study of designing a water ride in an amusement park. The main reason that this is here is so that you can see how to collect evidence about your work and how to present the project to get the maximum marks. There are also hints explaining what the teacher will be looking for when they come to mark the work.

Things to look for in Project 1:
- How the leaflet is laid out.
- What the teacher is looking for.
- The marking criteria for Levels 4, 5 and 6.
- What else was handed in.

Things to look for in Project 2:
- How the work is laid out.
- What evidence helps the teacher award a good mark.
- What needs to be handed in.
- How to plan a major project.

Project 1 – producing a leaflet

The leaflet that you will produce is about a subject that you are studying. You are going to hand it to parents at parents' evening. The skills and knowledge that you will need are:

- understanding corporate images
- designing leaflet templates
- choosing and designing logos
- capturing images
- making a folded leaflet.

It is possible that at the end of this project, all you will hand in is the finished leaflet, so it is important that you show that you have learned all of these skills in producing the final leaflet.

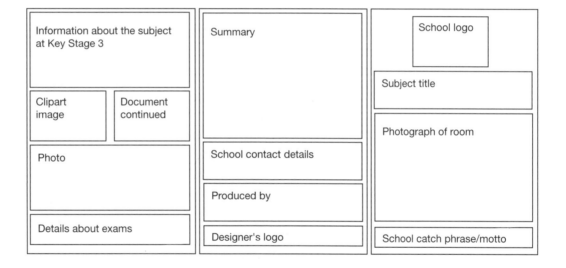

It would be good if you could produce a design template and hand this in as well. This would prove that you have planned out your pages carefully.

It's a good idea to make a list of criteria as to what makes a good leaflet and tick off what you have achieved.

Is it clear and easy to read? ☐
Is it suitable for the required audience? ☐
Does it fulfil its purpose? ☐
Is it uncluttered? ☐
Are the colours relevant? ☐
Do the colours go together? ☐
Is the font appropriate? ☐
Are the photographs clear? ☐
Are they appropriate? ☐

If you can answer yes to all these questions, you are probably going to get a reasonable mark.

How the work is marked

The target mark for this assignment is Level 4. If you complete all aspects of the assignment and produce a piece of work that is suitable for the audience and purpose, you have achieved Level 4.

The difference between Level 4 and Level 5 work when it comes to exchanging information is that you need to show clear awareness of audience. The best way to do this is to produce a second leaflet for a different audience, perhaps the Year 6 pupils. You will also need to hand in a list of reasons why each leaflet is different (for example, more pictures, larger text, more cartoon style pictures, brighter colours). This will show that you have thought about the audience and are aware of the needs of different audiences.

To get a Level 6, you need to show progression through the work. This means that you will need to hand in a lot more printouts. You need to produce printouts showing each stage of the design with alternatives at each stage. A good example of this would be:

I looked at putting these two pictures in my leaflet. I felt that the first was less appropriate as you couldn't see the computers very well.

A different example is shown opposite. The final printout is the same as before except that the font is different in this design. You need to explain why the font you used was more appropriate.

In this design I used Arial black font. I felt that this made the words too dark and I felt that this made the leaflet look less professional. I chose to use Palatino Linotype font as this looked much cleaner and clearer.

This needs to be done at every stage of the production of the leaflet so that progression is clearly shown. A series of printouts showing how the leaflet was made and what decisions were made along the way gives the teacher evidence that you are producing work with aspects of Level 6.

If you want to see the criteria that the teachers use for marking levels, visit the National Curriculum website (www.nc.uk.net/index.html).

It is important to think about what level work you are aiming for when you start. Ask your teacher what you need to do to get a higher level if you want to go for it.

Key Stage 3

This is where the majority of the skills teaching is done. Your child will learn how to use all the main applications by doing projects using them. They will also be taught how to produce good looking documents and how to make them suitable for the audience targeted and how to design them so that they are appropriate for the purpose. Every child will sit an exam at the end of each school year.

While the set the child is in will not depend on their exam mark, it does give a good indication of how they are doing. One report is produced for parents each year.

There will be exams in ICT at the end of each year and a SAT exam in year 9.

The ICT department has changed dramatically over the last few years. All suites now run Microsoft XP and Office XP. There are two rooms for teaching GCSE ICT, all pupils will study ICT throughout the school, you can opt for GCSE, but do not have to study it at this level.

Acorn School,
Oak Tree Hill,
Winchester
Hampshire
SO55 5SS

Tel: 0555 555555

PRODUCED BY:

JOE BLOGGS – 7CG

BLOGGS PRODUCTION

ACORN SCHOOL

Information and Communication Technology

'Always be careful using the Internet – Never give out personal details'

Project 2 – designing a theme park ride (Year 9)

This project is one of the three that are provided to teachers as part of the Key Stage 3 Framework for teaching ICT capability. The aim is to give an example of how you might complete the project, and emphasis is put on the things that need to be included but are often missed out. This is only one way to complete the project. Your school may or may not look at it, but the principles will be the same.

You are asked to design a water-based ride to be installed at a theme park. The ride must involve boats or rafts that move safely through a water channel, under computer control. Tenders have been invited for this ride and the bid must be in by the deadline. All bids must include:

- a schematic diagram of the ride
- a complete control system for the ride containing one or more boats
- a presentation to the park manager outlining the features of the ride and how safety features have been included in the system.

Ongoing evaluation, review and documentation are key features of this work.

First we need to break the project down into tasks. The first mistake pupils often make is to begin the schematic diagram now. It is important that you do your planning first. One of the best ways to do this is with a Gantt chart (there are lots of other ways). To make sure that you understand everything that is to be done, re-read the project brief and highlight the key points.

What to do

You are asked to design a water-based ride to be installed at a theme park. The ride must involve boats or rafts that move safely through a water channel, under computer control. Tenders have been invited for this ride and the bid must be in by the deadline. All bids must include:

- a schematic diagram of the ride
- a complete control system for the ride containing one or more boats
- a presentation to the park manager outlining the features of the ride and how safety features have been included in the system.

Ongoing evaluation, review and documentation are key features of this work.

Now that we have highlighted the key points, we can make sure that we focus on these and don't spend too much time on irrelevant tasks. The next phase is to plan what you are going to do when. This should only be done once. It can be adapted but don't spend lots of time making the Gantt chart look pretty.

A Gantt chart is simply a chart to show what tasks need to be done when. It helps you make sure that you are on track to meet the deadline. The Gantt chart below is created using Microsoft Excel.

Gantt chart for Theme park ride project

	1	2	3	4	5	6	7	8	9	10
Plan the project and brainstorm ideas	■									
Design theme park ride (schematic diagram)		■	■							
Write programs to control ride (in sections)				■	■					
Put sections of ride together						■				
Add in safety features							■			
Create presentation to park manager								■	■	
Listen to and evaluate others' presentations										■

Some Gantt charts can have a number of tasks being done at the same time (if there are a number of people to carry out the tasks or if some are ongoing). In this case, you can only do one thing at a time. You need to explain why you have produced the Gantt chart in this way, giving reasons for any choice.

I decided to produce a Gantt chart to make sure that I completed all the tasks on time. I felt that this was a good way of doing it as the chart is very clear about what needs to be done when. It is very important to plan the project carefully so I allocated one whole lesson for doing this, so that the plan is not rushed and I will have a good chance to get it right. Designing the ride will probably take more than one lesson, especially as I intend to brainstorm all my ideas first. I have therefore allowed two lessons for this. I have not used Flowol very much so will probably need two lessons to make the control system work and further lessons to add safety features and get it working properly. The presentation is fairly simple. I have used PowerPoint many times before and know that I can make it look good fairly quickly. I have allowed two lessons for this, which might give me some catch-up time if I need it.

This piece of writing clearly explains about the Gantt chart, so now you can begin to think about the brainstorm. If you have mind-mapping software, this will help to do it quickly. The software used for the mind map below is Mindmanager 4.0, although a perfectly adequate brainstorm can be achieved adding text to boxes in Microsoft Word.

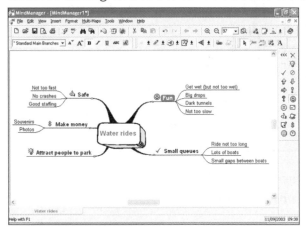

You need to explain briefly what the purpose of the brainstorm was and why it was useful. What have you gained by doing it?

A brainstorm is a very good way of getting ideas down on paper. We wanted to think of all the good things about water rides at theme parks so we could decide which features to include on our ride. We came up with a long list of ideas and can now refer back to this list when we are designing the ride. I could have produced the brainstorm just as quickly using pen and paper but I decided to use Mindmanager software because this would be easier to edit and easier to read. Also, I could print off more copies if I lost the original.

It's always a good idea to explain why you used the software that you did and to mention why you didn't use other methods. This shows the teacher that you are thinking about what you are doing.

Now that you have done all this, you have a really good idea of what you are about to do. You have now got to the point where you can produce your schematic diagram. This is basically a drawing of what you want your ride to do. It will help you when you come to write the program. A good schematic diagram should be clear and well annotated so that it is obvious what everything does.

After producing the brainstorm, I needed to look at the features to decide which ones I would include. The ride obviously needs to be safe, but also fun. The drops will give the feeling of excitement as there is a real sense of speed. The sprinkler will get people wet and could be a good surprise feature. The water jets will look really impressive and encourage people to get on the ride in the first place. Finally, a camera that takes people's photo on a down flume will give them the opportunity to buy a souvenir of the ride, reminding them so that they might want to come back, advertising it to their friends and also helping to increase profits at the theme park.

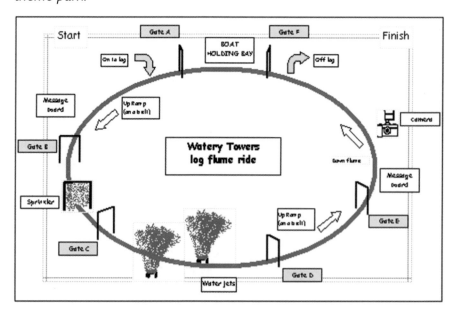

I spent some time making this look good (unlike the Gantt chart and the brainstorm) because this is a required part of the tender.

This is good – the teacher will be impressed because you have referred back to the project brief and explained why this has taken more effort and time than the other tasks.

Now might also be a good time to refer back to your Gantt chart and see that you are still on track. You should be doing this all the way through, but it wouldn't hurt to comment on it occasionally.

Looking at the Gantt chart, I am slightly ahead of the plan so I can really spend some time getting the program correct. I am still a bit unsure about using Flowol so I am going to write out the instructions on paper first. I have plenty of time to do this and it might even save time in the long run. I started to produce the plan and it was becoming huge. I found out that if I break the system down into sub-routines, it is much easier to manage and I can test each sub-routine one at a time.

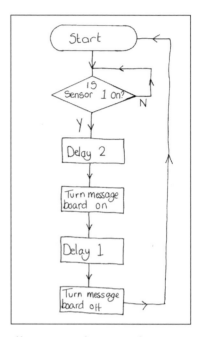

Now that the plan looks correct on paper, I will try to make it work using Flowol. I'm using this software because I have used it before and I know that it will run the computer program the way I want it to. There is another program at the school that I could use but I have never used it. Before starting I'm going to go back to the schematic diagram to adapt it and make it very detailed for the section that this part of the routine is looking at.

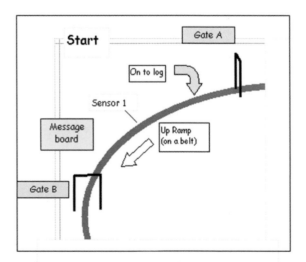

Now I have a better understanding of what will happen in this sub-routine, I can use Flowol to try to make it work.

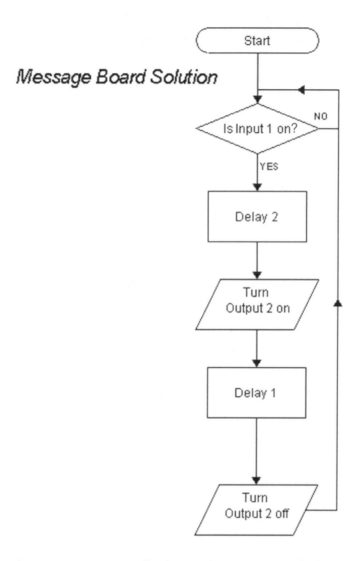

Message Board Solution

This is progressing well. The teacher is aware of what you are doing, of the choices you have made and why you have made them. Obviously, you will need to include a similar section for each part of the system. Use this as the template for the other sections and try to get each working. When they are all finished and tested, you can combine them to make one large system that runs using each sub-routine in the correct order.

Now the system is up and running, you might be tempted to spend too long playing with it and showing it off (because you are so proud of it), so be aware of this. You should run the system to check that it works as a whole and look at how to refine it if it does run properly.

I performed a test run on the system and it worked very well. I had made a mistake because I had forgotten to turn the message board on in the program (even though it was on my hand-written plan). I fixed this problem quickly by altering the flowchart and decided to look at the timings to see if they needed refining.

This has overcome a major problem for the teacher. You need to show evidence that you have improved your work, but normally all the teacher has to go on is the finished project (which works). You have explained a slight error and what you did to fix it. Refining is the next point – it is one way of reviewing your work as well as a way of improving the system.

An important part of the system is the timing. If the delays are too short, boats might get stuck in the gates and they might crash into each other. If the delays are too long, the queues will build up too much, so less people will go on the ride and parts of the ride could become boring if you are waiting too long for something to happen. I adapted the timings because I felt that there was not enough time for the boat to pass through the first gate. I changed the delay from 5 seconds to 10 seconds. I felt that there was too long between one boat and the next being released so I changed the delay for this from 1 minute to 30 seconds. This means that twice as many boats can leave in the same time, keeping the queues down. One boat should be about halfway round when the next leaves.

This has explained changes to the system (more marks) and has also made some predictions – you can test these later if there is time. The system should now work as you want it.

The final stage of the project is the presentation. It is important to make clear the purpose of the presentation and the audience. You can then explain the choices you made about the presentation – for example, why you chose this particular order of slides and how you designed the presentation for the audience.

The presentation is a very important part of the project, as it is this that will help win the bid for the water ride. The purpose of the presentation is to persuade the park manager that this ride would be a worthwhile investment for their park. The target audience is a professional businessperson so I should avoid silly images and do not need to produce fancy colourful text at the expense of getting the information across. It needs to look professional and should still be eye-catching. I am going to try to avoid too much clutter on each slide. I want the key points to be emphasised really clearly and it does not really matter how many slides there are. I want to try to avoid the presentation taking too long as I don't want to bore the park manager – they are probably very busy and will be thinking about getting on with other things. I will keep the style of each slide the same so that there are no occasions when the park manager will look at the design rather than the information on the slide. For this reason I am going to produce a master slide.

This means that all the slides I produce will automatically have this style. I have decided that the slides should be the following.

1. *A title slide.*

2. *What I am trying to achieve.*

3. *The schematic diagram.*

4. *Some photos of what the ride might look like (taken from similar rides, sources are from home and the Internet).*

5. *A summary explaining the benefits to the park of having this ride.*

Before I started making the actual presentation I thought about the criteria that make a presentation good. The obvious factors are that it needs to be designed for the correct audience and the purpose of the presentation should be clear. The presentation will need to be easy to edit as it is possible that the park manager might want to show it to other people, such as a group of children who might use the ride. Each slide needs to have a lot of white space around the information to make it stand out. The text should be big enough to read and should not clash or blend in too much with the background. Any images should be clear and easy to see. Too low a resolution might make the quality poor. I have decided to add a commentary to the presentation and set the show up so that it will move from one slide to the next automatically. This is because I can then give the park manager a copy and they can run through it in their own time without me being there. I have seen many presentations that have lots of animations and large images, and this can mean that they run quite slowly. This would reduce the impact of the presentation, so I will therefore try to avoid overfilling the presentation with these.

Now you have explained what you are about to do, you can do it.

Watery Towers log flume

By Dave and Max

What I am trying to achieve

- We have designed a water park ride

- It needed to be:
  – Fun
  – Safe
  – Needs to make money.

How the ride will run

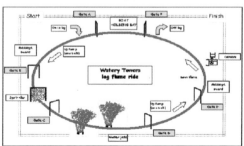

What will it look like?

Here are some images found searching using www.google.com that show how dramatic log flumes can be

How will the ride benefit the park?

- Increase to number of rides.
- Be a new style of ride.
- Add more selling points (Photograph)
- Reduce waiting time on other rides.
- Encourage return visits.

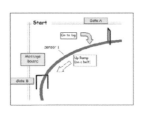

Your work is almost complete. Some pupils stop at this point, but if you refer back to your highlighted project brief and the Gantt chart, you will see that we need to evaluate the project.

The most common error is to write about how well you have done. This is not the time to write, 'I feel that I have worked really hard and done really well on this project and hit all my deadlines'. The evaluation is about the project; the teacher expects you to have worked really hard.

I found this project challenging but I am pleased with the result. The aim was to produce a schematic diagram, working control system and presentation to market a water ride. The documentation I have produced that goes along with the work, explains very clearly the decisions that I have made and why I made them. This has achieved its purpose. The schematic diagram is clear and gives a good idea of what the ride will be like, and I feel that this too has achieved its purpose. The presentation was easy to produce but needed to be suitable for a very specific audience. I also felt that it was important to make the presentation portable and easy to edit for future use with other audiences.

The most difficult part of this project for me was actually making the control system. I have become much more proficient in using the Flowol software and managed to produce a working system once I had broken down the jobs into sub-routines. At first, I tried to make one large program but this was very difficult to follow. I had to remember where I was the whole time to test each part of the system. The sub-routines were much easier to work out, and once I had planned them on paper by breaking down the schematic diagram into sections it was much easier.

This is good so far. You have explained a few problems and how you overcame them, now you need to explain what you would do differently next time, or what you have taken on board to do again next time.

Next time I do a similar project I will spend at least as much time planning the work. I feel that it really helped having the Gantt chart to keep track of what happens next and it was good writing all the ideas down in a brainstorm – I never forgot what I was doing from one lesson to the next. I think it was very useful planning the control system on paper first. Next time I think I will plan time to do this rather than hoping that I was ahead of schedule as I was this time.

This makes for quite a good project. You have hit most of the aspects of Level 6 and, most importantly, you have good evidence to show this.

Answers

Chapter 1

1 i   the reading age of the guests
   ii   needs to be bright, happy and fun
   iii a relevant layout for an invitation

2 i   relevant images
   ii   appropriate for 15 year olds
   iii clear eye-catching title
   iv   not so cluttered
   v   more information needed to explain location and time

3 a   Anyone can write a website and they might make mistakes or mislead you.

   b   *Any three from:*
        i   The URL will normally be a more suitable name on an official site.
        ii   An official site is more likely to be correct (be aware that any site could say that it is official in the short term).
        iii The other information and links will help you establish how reliable the site is.
        iv   A site with more adverts is likely to be less reliable.

4 *Any two from:*
   i   to help convince people that their argument is correct
   ii   to try to cover up facts that they would rather not be made public
   iii to distract the attention from other issues

5 *Any two from:*
   i   the reading age of the document
   ii   the colour of the text and background
   iii how cluttered the page is
   iv   how large the font is

Chapter 2

1 *Any one from:*
   i   Search engines do not search the whole Internet, they stop after a certain amount of time so might not find the same sites.
   ii   Search engines search in different ways so would find different sites.
   iii Some search engines are specifically linked to some sites (you can ask the search engine to find your site).

2 *One from*
   i   to recognise the author of the work/photographer and give them credit *or*
   ii   so that you can find it again

3 *Any three from:*
   i   change the scale so that it looks the way you want it to
   ii   only select certain data when creating the graph to ignore unwanted data
   iii choose the style of graph which shows your data in as good a light as possible
   iv   add another line to the graph that compares unfavourably to your data

Chapter 3

1 *Any three from:*
   i   saves space
   ii   easy to transfer
   iii easy to edit

iv easy to backup

v can be accessed from anywhere on a network

v) portable

vi easy to sort

2 *Any three from:*

i relevance of data to your work

ii Data Protection Act 1998

iii whether to use a tally or questionnaire

iv how you are going to store the information

v what the purpose of the questionnaire is

3 *Any three from:*

i can be edited easily

ii similar calculations can be repeated easily

iii can be saved and reopened

iv you can see a lot more information

v graphs can be produced

vi formulae can be used

vii can be used to simulate situations

Chapter 4

1 **i** Tasks can be done while the operator is not there.

ii Computers can perform tasks very quickly.

2 **i** You might decide that you do not start at the beginning, one task might be more appropriate to start with even though it would be used later in the system.

ii You might decide to set yourself deadlines to meet so that you finish the task by the deadline.

3 **i** To perform routine tasks quickly and efficiently.

Chapter 5

1 **i** *One mark* for spotting that the beans may not be ready when they are served,

ii *One mark* for adding a loop to correct it.

2 *At least three from:*

i click on Record new macro

ii click on a cell in the required column

iii click on the Sort button

iv click on Stop recording

3 **a** mail merge

b *Any four from:*

i create a list of names and addresses

ii create a letter in a word processor

iii click on tools, Mail merge and set up the page

iv insert merge fields

v merge the information

Chapter 6

1 **i** temperature sensor in the oven (will keep temperature constant)

ii accurate weights / measurements

iii accurate timer

2 **i** fd 50 rt 90 fd 75 rt 90 fd 50 rt 90 fd 75 bk 25 rt 90 fd 50 rt 90 fd 25 rt 90 fd 50

ii same but with forward, backward and right

iii same drawn in reverse (backward, forward and left)

3   *Any five from:*
  i   sensors don't need breaks
  ii   sensors always take the measurements on time
  iii   sensors can work without the operator present
  iv   data can be transferred to computer easily
  v   easy to draw graphs
  vi   data is easily saved without taking up much space
  vii   sensors can measure very accurately

Chapter 7

1   a   i   left aligned
        ii   correct spacing
        iii   no punctuation in the addresses
        iv   standard font
        v   header used where appropriate

    b   hand-written letter will have:
    Any three from:
        i   address on top right hand side
        ii   indented paragraphs
        iii   punctuation on address and after Dear Sir/Madam
        iv   not necessarily left aligned (less information on the page)

2   i   young child – bright colours
    ii   sports club member – relevant pictures
    iii   professional – more text than image
    iv   teenager – catchy title

3   So you can clearly see if the target has been achieved.
    Any two from:
    i   appropriate language for audience (check by readability score)
    ii   spelled correctly
    iii   90% of the page covered or any other similar

Chapter 8

1   *Any five from:*
    i   scanned photo
    ii   draw in a graphic package
    iii   copy from the Internet
    iv   import from a digital camera
    v   clipart
    vi   scan from a book
    vii   screen grab

2   *Any two from:*
    i   if it is all at the bottom or top the page will look unbalanced
    ii   it can emphasise important points by surrounding them
    iii   it can give the reader a break from too much text

3   i   newspaper front page – desktop publisher
    ii   letter – word processor
    iii   cash flow forecast – spreadsheet
    iv   presentation – slide show software

4   *Any three from:*
    i   processor speed
    ii   software loaded on machine
    iii   memory on hard drive
    iv   RAM
    v   graphics card in the monitor
    vi   peripherals available (e.g. scanner)

Chapter 9

1 a A jpeg is a smaller file, so takes up less space on the hard drive.

  b *Any three from:*
    i when you are transferring the file
    ii when you are saving it on to a portable drive or disk
    iii when you do not need high quality
    iv when the hard drive is nearly full

2 *Any three from:*
  i not everyone is who they say they are, people might abuse the information
  ii you might start getting inappropriate junk mail
  iii credit card fraud
  iv possibility of drawing unwanted attention from stalkers

3 *Any three from:*
  i immediate communications
  ii working from home
  iii file transferring
  iv time wasted by employees with personal emails
  v saves money on postage
  vi increases pressure because deadlines are tighter and there is no excuse 'the cheque is in the post'
  vii unfair on small businesses with no computers

Multiple choice answers

Chapter 1
1: B **2**: C **3**: C **4**: D **5**: C

Chapter 2
1: B **2**: C **3**: B **4**: C **5**: A

Chapter 3
1: C **2**: C **3**: C **4**: C **5**: D

Chapter 4
1: C **2**: B **3**: D **4**: B

Chapter 5
1: A **2**: A **3**: C **4**: B **5**: C **6**: D

Chapter 6
1: D **2**: D **3**: A **4**: D **5**: A

Chapter 7
1: B **2**: A **3**: A **4**: B **5**: C

Chapter 8
1: B **2**: C **3**: A **4**: A **5**: B

Chapter 9
1: C **2**: D **3**: B **4**: D **5**: B

Index

Acknowledgements

The author and publisher are grateful to the copyright holders, as credited, for permission to use quoted materials and photographs.

Toys R Us page 9.
Screenshots used by permission from Microsoft Corporation.

Every effort has been made to trace the copyright holders and to obtain their permission for the use of copyright material. The author and publisher will gladly receive information enabling them to rectify any error or omission in subsequent editions.

Letts Educational
The Chiswick Centre
414 Chiswick High Road
London W4 5TF

Tel: 0845 602 1937
Fax: 020 8742 8767
Email: mail@lettsed.co.uk
Website: www.Letts-SuccessZone.com

First published 2004, 2005

10 9 8 7 6 5 4 3

Text © Max Begley and David Sadler 2004

British Library Cataloging in Publication Data. A CIP record of this book is available from the British Library.

ISBN 184315 271 1

Letts Educational Limited is a division of Granada Learning Limited, part of Granada plc.

Prepared by *specialist* publishing services ltd, Milton Keynes

Printed in Italy